LOURDES

LOURDES

Font of Faith, Hope, and Charity

Elizabeth Ficocelli

FOREWORD BY
Fr. Benedict J. Groeschel, CFR

Paulist Press
New York/Mahwah, NJ

Credits for the cover and interior illustrations are on page 179.

The Scripture quotations contained herein are from the New Revised Standard Version: Catholic Edition Copyright © 1989 and 1993, by the Division of Christian Education of the National Council of the Churches of Christ in the United States of America. Used by permission. All rights reserved.

Cover design by Sharyn Banks
Book design by Lynn Else

Library of Congress Cataloging-in-Publication Data

Ficocelli, Elizabeth.
    Lourdes : font of faith, hope, and charity / Elizabeth Ficocelli ; foreword by Benedict J. Groeschel.
        p. cm.
    Includes bibliographical references.
    ISBN-13: 978-0-8091-4486-0 (alk. paper)
    1. Mary, Blessed Virgin, Saint—Apparitions and miracles—France—Lourdes. 2. Bernadette, Saint, 1844–1879. 3. Lourdes (France)—Religious life and customs. 4. Lourdes (France)—Description and travel. 5. Christian pilgrims and pilgrimages—France—Lourdes. 6. Christian shrines—France—Lourdes. 7. Lourdes, Our Lady of. I. Title.
    BT653.F48 2007
    232.91'7094478—dc22

                                                                    2007017003

Published by Paulist Press
997 Macarthur Boulevard
Mahwah, New Jersey 07430

www.paulistpress.com

Printed and bound in the
United States of America

CONTENTS

Photographs appear on pages 81–90.

For my father, Verner Ahles,
and for all God's children
who suffer from illness and disability
E. F.

For I will take you from the nations,
and gather you from all the countries,
and bring you into your own land.
I will sprinkle clean water upon you,
and you shall be clean from all your uncleannesses,
and from all your idols
I will cleanse you. A new heart I will give you,
and a new spirit I will put within you;
and I will remove from your body the heart of stone
and give you a heart of flesh.

Ezekiel 36:24–26

FOREWORD

Fr. Benedict J. Groeschel, CFR

When I was asked to introduce Elizabeth Ficocelli's new book about Lourdes, I knew immediately that I was intended to discharge a debt. Only three years ago I had awoken from unconsciousness after three weeks in critical condition as a result of a near-fatal car accident. I would learn then that there was no medical explanation for my survival because I had gone for a half hour without any vital signs. The attending physicians were sure that I would not live or, if I did live, that I would never regain my mental abilities. For months after my waking, they doubted I would ever walk again. I lay in my hospital bed for another six weeks, unable to move or speak, breathing with a respirator, and having use only of my left arm.

As I struggled to comprehend my situation, I immediately placed my complete recovery in the hands of Our Lady of Lourdes and made Saint Bernadette my special intercessor. Without the slightest hesitation, I consider my case to be one of the miracles given to those who did not actually go to the shrine, a place of miracles and healings. [In Fr. Groeschel's case, this means someone who did not go to Lourdes at the *actual time of need,* as he had already visited the shrine years earlier.—Ed.] In God's Providence many blessings and healings are often given to sick people through Our Lady even though they may not have visited the shrine. I am in the strange category of those whose experience qualifies as a medical miracle but not as a church miracle. Why? Because I have yet to meet a physician informed about my condition who would be prepared to say that my recovery was anything less than a miracle. Because my recovery was gradual and incomplete in some ways, it would not be considered by the Medical Bureau of Lourdes.

In the first moments of regaining memory and consciousness, there came to my mind the photograph of "la petite Soubirous" and also her miraculously preserved body at the Sisters of Charity motherhouse at Nevers. My first attempts at coherent communication were with a priest-friend who had once accompanied me on a pilgrimage to Lourdes and Nevers and who had prayed for me from the first moment after learning of my encounter with the front bumper of an automobile. After news of the accident was released, Father John Lynch and David Burns, my fellow travelers, were joined by a large number of people of many religions who prayed for me in the critical hours and days that followed. When I awoke, I turned to God, our blessed Savior, His blessed Mother, and Saint Bernadette, and I have continued to ask Saint Bernadette's assistance every day. I have been able to return to my duties and find that in my old age I am even busier than ever.

Friends have been eager to send me back to Lourdes. I would cherish such a visit, but I would be disinclined to ask for a complete recovery. I still have some physical handicaps, which will probably be with me when I am called home to God. If the Lord had wanted me to recover completely, He could easily have brought it about, but He left me moderately incapacitated for His purposes. I see my remaining injuries as a blessing. I understand Bernadette's words to those who wanted to take her to be healed at Lourdes when she was dying. She responded very firmly that the spring was not for her.

Now for this book. The author has provided a very readable and up-to-date account of the complex phenomenon called Lourdes. From the first mystical experience of the little street child, to the moving visit of Pope John Paul II toward the end of his life (his last trip abroad), the author has described and integrated the many aspects of Lourdes.

A number of competent writers in the past have attempted to do the same, giving their own point of view. Some focused their attention on healings and miracles, while others tried to analyze various political forces that took advantage of the shrine and its great multitude of believers. Some became involved in the mythology that inevitably comes to surround an authentic theophany, or manifestation of the divine. Others stress what might be called the sociological and historical aspects of the Lourdes phenomenon. Almost all writers treat with great respect the little peasant girl who, in the midst of the excitement that accompanies reports of a vision, faithfully and quietly fulfilled her task of communicating the Blessed Virgin's message— prayer and penance.

There are many accounts of individual experiences at Lourdes. One well-known but often-overlooked author, Dr. Alexis Carrel, a Nobel Prize winner in medicine (1912), has left a moment-by-moment record of a miraculous healing that he observed at Lourdes in 1902.* And Franz Werfel, a Jewish refugee hiding in Lourdes from the Nazis and their French allies, published a fictionalized account of the visionary's life as *The Song of Bernadette,* very popular in this country in the 1940s and 1950s.** The book led to the pro-

---

* See Alexis Carrel, *The Voyage to Lourdes,* trans. Virgilia Peterson (New York: Harper and Brothers, 1950; reprinted Real-View-Books, 1994).

** This book is still in print (Fort Collins, CO: Ignatius Press, 2006).

duction of one of the most celebrated and popular films ever made.

Elizabeth Ficocelli's book successfully brings those interested in Lourdes up to date. It is an indispensable guide for anyone going to the shrine who wishes to be informed. The author explores both the history of Lourdes and the many practical aspects of the shrine, like understanding the remarkable and complex volunteer services available gratis to pilgrims of many nationalities. Those who go to Lourdes uninformed about what is available will nonetheless be taken care of. However, they may well miss many things that they ought to see and come to appreciate. The author precisely describes the many fascinating aspects of the Lourdes experience.

I found her chapter on the priests who work at Lourdes to be very moving and interesting. She puts faces on the clergy and lay volunteers, who in self-effacing ways keep this very complex series of services to millions of people running so smoothly. I had met some priests assigned there, but I did not know much about them, where they came from, or why they were working there. Obviously the author has spent time with them and was very impressed with their spiritual motives for serving at the shrine, which is surely a demanding apostolate. Their principal responsibility is to see that the request of the Blessed Virgin to Bernadette is fulfilled: that prayer for sinners and personal repentance accompany the pilgrim to Lourdes. After I read the account of the priests in chapter 8, I thought that this poor French peasant girl had certainly accomplished the task she was given through a mystical apparition by the banks of the Gave.

Unfortunately, the largely illusory debate between religion and natural science is back in the media. Lourdes and the miracles and blessings associated with it again take on a special relevance. Here is a place where medical science and fervent religious faith actually encounter each other. Repeatedly and with no real success at all, those who are hostile to religion, or at least uninvolved in faith and religious experience, have tried to dismiss the inexplicable cures that have occurred there since the days of the apparitions 150 years ago. This has caused church authorities to be extremely narrow and careful in identifying genuine cures. There is a vast disproportion between the number of cures and recoveries reported and the small list of miracles actually certified and accepted. This does not mean that other miracles did not happen. This book carefully explains how the bishops and staff are working to maintain the strictest scientific evaluation and also to recognize the favors and blessings reported by large numbers of pilgrims and devotees, some of whom, like me, are from far away.

As you begin this latest account on Lourdes, one aimed at accuracy and completeness, I would suggest that you begin to read prayerfully. Even if you are somewhat skeptical, put yourself in a prayerful frame of mind. We are psychologically unaccustomed to dealing with such phenomena; consequently, our minds may reject unthinkingly what goes beyond our comprehension. Lourdes is mysterious; it is not superstition. Lourdes is miraculous; it is not hysterical. Lourdes has survived endless attempts to undermine its authenticity. Even today it represents for millions a place where divine power and providence operate through the sacred shrine of the Holy Virgin and the humble peasant girl kneeling at her feet.

Fr. Benedict Groeschel is a well-known author and psychologist who has written on spirituality, mystical phenomena, and private revelations.

PREFACE

The invitation to write a book on Lourdes to commemorate the 150th anniversary of the apparitions came from my publisher, Paulist Press, in March 2006, as my husband and I were about to slip away for some much needed time in the wooded hills of southeastern Ohio. To be truthful, I was hesitant about taking on the project for two reasons. One, I had never been to Lourdes, which I felt was essential in order to do the book justice. Two, I was under the impression that a great number of books had already been written on the subject. What could I possibly offer that would be new and different? I promised my editor, Susan Heyboer O'Keefe, that I would pray about it. At the time, my heart was already fixed on a new book for Catholic teenagers, and I wanted to be sure that the Lourdes opportunity was truly God's plan rather than a distraction from my current endeavors. The day before leaving for the cabin, I hastened the discernment process by asking for a sign. God, always gracious, complied. In response to a quick Google search on Lourdes, I found to my surprise that the Sanctuary* was making newspaper headlines around the world. According to the reports, the bishop and medical director were proposing important revisions to the tradi-

---

* The term *sanctuary* indicates a sacred place of pilgrimage, often a building or church. At Lourdes, the original sanctuary was the chapel built above the grotto. Later on, the multiplicity of churches and basilicas resulted in renaming the whole area "the Sanctuaries." For simplicity, however, I refer to Lourdes as the Sanctuary throughout this book.

tional method of reporting, analyzing, and documenting inexplicable cures widely associated with Lourdes in order to facilitate the determination of miracles. *Well, I thought to myself, this was news.* It was sign enough for me, and I accepted the assignment. God would have to work out the other details.

It did not take me long in my research process to learn about Marlene Watkins, the woman responsible for starting Our Lady of Lourdes North American Volunteers. She was a delight to speak with and a veritable wealth of information for the book. Marlene, like so many others, encouraged me to make my own pilgrimage to Lourdes, and for the first time on the project I felt an inner urging to join this particular group. Unfortunately, their remaining monthly pilgrimages were completely booked. Marlene assured me calmly that if the Blessed Mother desired my husband and me to come to Lourdes, something would work out—it always did. The itinerary that sounded particularly interesting to me was their October special needs pilgrimage. It presented a unique opportunity to meet and travel with people with illness and disability as well as those volunteers prepared to serve them and others like them at Lourdes. Since my husband works with people with disabilities for a living, the match seemed perfect. The possibility of "something working out" prompted me to update our passports, just in case. After all, if God was going to open a door, we needed to be prepared to walk through it. Sure enough, two cancellations occurred on the October pilgrimage, and a few weeks later my husband and I found ourselves on an Air France flight bound for Paris. A second flight to the southern city of Pau, followed by a forty-five-minute bus ride, would complete our journey to our final destination of Lourdes.

My purpose in Lourdes was twofold. First and foremost, I was traveling as a pilgrim to delve into the experience of what had happened at this holy place in 1858, and to witness firsthand the impact of these apparitions on the Church and on the world. Second, I was in Lourdes as an investigative journalist to complete a manuscript that was nearly two-thirds written. Through Marlene, I would have the pleasure and privilege to meet Father Régis-Marie de La Teyssonnière, author, lecturer, and world-renowned authority on Bernadette and her apparitions. This knowledgeable priest willingly agreed to review my manuscript for accuracy, as distorted information has been a persistent plague to Lourdes since the apparitions began. God's answer to my second concern was beginning to reveal itself. While it's true that a great deal has been written on Lourdes, not that much has been written in English, and what is currently available is often tainted with inaccurate details to downright skepticism. The door was wide open for a believing Catholic to recount in English an accurate and up-to-date presentation on Lourdes, complete with its important spiritual ramifications for today.

So many people made this book possible, and for that I thank them sincerely. Marlene Watkins and, of course, Father de La Teyssonnière provided me with extraordinary help. Father de La Teyssonnière, together with the Lourdes Communications Department, was instrumental in making it possible for an otherwise unknown American author to meet with several key people at the Sanctuary to glean their important perspectives. Thus I would like to extend my sincere gratitude to these gentlemen by name, who were both gracious and informative: Monsignor Jacques Perrier, bishop of Tarbes and Lourdes; Father Raymond Zambelli, rector; Father Patrick-Louis Desprez, general chaplain of the Hospitality of Our Lady of Lourdes; Dr. Patrick Theillier, medical director; Mr. Gabriel Barbry, former president of Hospitality; Mr. Philippe Tardy-Joubert, International

Hospitality Conference coordinator; Father Liam Griffin, Father Marcel Emard Duguay, and Brother François Sainte-Marie, chaplains; and Mr. Pierre Adias, communications director. Finally, I would also like to thank Agnès Baranger and Danielle Sempéré in Communications for their invaluable assistance as well.

Introduction

A PERSONAL EXPERIENCE OF LOURDES

It was a challenge at times during my own trip to Lourdes to have to change roles from being a pilgrim one minute to a journalist the next. More than once, my husband and I had to run, literally, from one location to another through the hilly terrain of the Sanctuary and the surrounding area to make an appointment or scheduled tour. Despite the frantic pace, we were both able to find a few precious hours to pray and simply experience Lourdes. At week's end, neither of us could have asked for a more meaningful experience.

The question that I was asked most after we returned home was this: Did you experience any miracles? And to that question I can emphatically answer *yes!* The whole experience for me was a miracle, starting with the unexpected assignment of a much-needed project to the opportunity to go and experience a place I could otherwise only dream about. Plus, there were lots of "little miracles" along the way. Two weeks before our departure, an incident from my youth suddenly found itself in the forefront of my conscience. It was something I had not thought about for years. But now, here it was, in all its ugliness, begging for release. When the priest accompanying our pilgrimage encouraged us in his very first homily at Lourdes to leave at this place anything we may have consciously or subconsciously buried from long ago, I didn't need to be invited twice. I made arrangements to meet with him that evening and made one of the most important confessions in my life.

This, I would come to discover, is a common scenario at Lourdes. Our Lady invites her children to this sacred shrine not for her sake, but in order to lead us to her Son. The Sacrament of Reconciliation is one of the ways she accomplishes this. The celebration of the Eucharist is another. Our pilgrimage group was able to experience the universal Church at the international Mass, as well as more intimate liturgies in sacred places in and around the Sanctuary, including the original chapel, the grotto, and the tiny room where Bernadette lived with her family in dire poverty. Mass in this latter place was particularly affecting. To me, there was a tangible power to this holy and humble room that had been blessed not only by the saint and her family, but also by the countless Masses offered on this very spot. With literally no room to kneel because of those already on their knees on either side of me, I was resigned to stand through Mass, and at times it was hard to keep from swaying as the waves of our prayers were lifted to heaven in English and Latin.

Another interesting event occurred one evening as we were participating in the Torchlight Procession along with thousands of other pilgrims. As we were rounding the circle at the end of the long esplanade, my husband and I were struck simultaneously by the thought of how awesome it must be to be one of the people leading the prayers on the steps of the Rosary Basilica. How must it feel, we wondered, to lead the Rosary in your native tongue, your voice ringing out across an endless sea of candles and throughout the entire Sanctuary? We were intrigued by this collective consciousness and even more amazed and delighted to discover ourselves doing this very act of service the following evening. As our voices proclaimed the reflections of the Glorious Mysteries in English to the multitude processing before us, I had a recollection. It was an expression frequently uttered that week by one of the endearing sisters on our pilgrimage, a woman who had every right to complain due to an illness that caused painful sores on her legs and prohibited her from walking. Instead, she was one of the happiest souls I have ever met. To coin the phrase, she would giggle at every juncture, "How great is that?" Well, Sister, this was more than great. It was simply glorious.

Then, there was the experience of the baths, or *piscines,* the place where pilgrims can immerse themselves in the water of the spring that Bernadette uncovered. Our pilgrimage director had made an appointment for our group in advance due to the demand of this activity, but there was a mix-up and it didn't look likely that the women at least were going to get in. The line to the baths was closed due to the exorbitant number of pilgrims and people who had been waiting for hours. I can't say that I wasn't disappointed, but I resigned myself to follow God's will and experience what He wanted me to. When I spotted a mother from our group taking her young son behind the curtained area to be bathed (people with disabilities are always escorted to the front of the line), I knelt down on the walkway outside the area of the *piscines* and prayed for them.

A few minutes later, I felt a tap on my shoulder. One of the sisters from our group told me that the confusion had been resolved and our appointment was being honored. Would I like to experience the baths? She led me inside the gate, past the guards, to a bench just outside one of the curtained areas. Instead of feeling exalted or important, I felt completely humbled and undeserving, and at once the tears began to flow. I don't think they stopped the whole time I went from that outside bench to the inside bench, to the curtained dressing area, or to the bath itself. But the Italian women working the *piscines* that day were most kind and patient with me. I'm not sure if it was the chilling effect of the spring water or the experience itself that literally took my breath away, but I came away from the baths revitalized and joyful and ever so peaceful.

Still another poignant moment was praying the petitions we had brought with us from home. Prior to our departure, we e-mailed everybody on our address lists that we would be happy to take their prayer petitions to the grotto at Lourdes. It was a moment of vulnerability, as we did not know how this offer would be received or even understood, but we were both amazed at the number of responses that flooded in. Many came from the most surprising sources. Neither one of us had really studied the petitions; we simply cut and pasted them together into a document to take to Lourdes. My husband read through them prayerfully while he was on the line for the men's baths. I took possession of the list later in the week.

Kneeling on the pavement in front of the grotto where Bernadette had her first apparition a century and a half before, I had the first opportunity to really absorb what people had entrusted us with. There were pages of prayers before me—prayers of thanksgiving and prayers of supplication. There were prayers for individual causes and prayers for the world. There were prayers for physical cures, for children to return to the faith, for employment, for spiritual and emotional healing. It took me three-quarters of an hour to pray these petitions before that grotto, because I was truly *praying* them. As I began to experience the hurt and the burdens and the fears of the people who had confided to us their deepest longings, tears flowed once again. I considered how big the shoulders and heart must be of our Savior who hears and answers all these prayers in a way that's best for each of us. Hard as it is to describe, I experienced a definite sense of listening at the grotto. These prayers were being heard in a powerful way, and I could only attribute that to the crowds of the faithful around me who were making the same heartfelt gesture.

Between the interviews that had been arranged for me and the tours of the Sanctuary, I was not able to do any real volunteering at Lourdes, as several of the people in our group had come to do. My husband, Mark, however, had the extraordinary opportunity to serve in the men's *piscines*. After filling out the necessary paperwork and receiving approval, he was sent to work the baths on Tuesday afternoon of our pilgrimage. Unfortunately, too many English-speaking workers were scheduled that day and he was not needed. Although Mark was disappointed, he left with a smile, trusting in the reality that God works in his own ways and in his own time. "The next day," he recalls, "Elizabeth was scheduled to interview Mr. Gabriel Barbry, whom we were told was a former president of Hospitality. So there we were, waiting in the volunteers' cafeteria for someone we didn't know, and to make matters worse, our translator had not shown up. At once, I saw a man with a very warm and welcoming face come through the line, being greeted by several people. I recognized him right away as the man in charge of the *piscines,* and something prompted me to ask him if he was Mr. Barbry. He was. I found myself feeling hopeful again that perhaps I could work the baths after all."

After a delightful interview that was aided by an impromptu translator who also volunteered in the baths, my husband told Mr. Barbry about not being able to serve at the *piscines* the previous day. The Frenchman jovially invited Mark to return to the baths that afternoon. He jumped at the chance, running all the way back to the hotel to change and down through the Sanctuary again to join the other men waiting for the "chef" of the *piscines* to assign them their duties. In moments, Mr. Barbry came out of the building to survey those who were waiting. As soon as he caught sight of Mark, his face lit up and his arms went out in greeting as he called him by name. Ahead of all the other men who were waiting, he took Mark in, treating him as if he were his own son. At first, he escorted the nervous American into one of the dressing areas for the *piscines* and in more French than English communicated to Mark to prepare to go into the baths. My husband immediately gestured back that he wanted to *work* the baths. Mr. Barbry understood and with a smile took him upstairs where the volunteers prepare to work. He took an apron and carefully tied it around my husband. Then he led Mark downstairs and found an English-speaking person to instruct him on all the nuances of working in the baths. Once all the volunteers had been selected, Mr. Barbry gathered everyone for a series of prayers and asked Mark to do the reading in English.

"I felt humbled to be given this honor to proclaim the Gospel to the men I'd be serving the pilgrims with that afternoon," says Mark. "When we finished our prayers I was assigned to a *piscine* and introduced to three Italians, a Frenchman, and an Englishman. My first job was to wrap a towel around a pilgrim before he went into the bath. When the first man came through my line, I remembered how I felt two days before when I experienced the baths. I couldn't help but notice how one of the Italian volunteers that day treated every detail of his service, whether it was assisting with a shoe or a sock or a hat, with a certain kind of reverence. It had made me feel special and cared for, and I tried to convey the same attitude as a volunteer. This is when the humility of this situation really hit me. These men would come into the bathing area in their undershorts. As I tried to create some discretion by holding the towel behind them so that they could shed their undergarments before I carefully wrapped them, I realized that there was a great humbleness in the activity, both for the man being assisted as well as for myself. There was an inherent trust, a give-and-take in that situation and in the decorum and demeanor of all of us who were volunteering that was so important to that experience."

The second task Mark was given was to assist with lowering pilgrims into the bath. Before this ritual, the pilgrim would issue his prayer, either silently or aloud. It was humbling for my husband to stand and pray alongside these men as they prayed in different languages, knowing that whether the prayers were in French or German or Italian or Croatian, they were all going to God. "The more I participated, the more I realized how trusting you had to be in this experience, to be fundamentally naked and in the literal hands of two complete strangers, giving total control of yourself to them as they lowered you down into the bath and prayed with you, trusting that they were there in support of you and your prayer intentions."

The last station Mark worked was the dressing area. Again he tried to emulate what he had witnessed during his own experience in the baths and performed his duties with the utmost care and respect. "It was amazing how even the simplest of tasks could seem to be so profound. It made me think about how it must have been when the Lord washed the apostles' feet. As a Catholic, I've been to Holy Thursday

Mass countless times. I've always thought of the priest washing someone's feet as a nice symbolic gesture, but I never felt engaged in the activity, either as an observer or a participant, as one of profound reverence and respect for another. Being in that dressing room and being able to help in these very small yet intimate ways with these total strangers really drove home the message of how service to others can be simple yet profound. That's the message I came away from Lourdes with, that it's about being of service to others, and that being of service to others is a gift to you as much as it is to them."

This is an insightful awareness for a man who's been giving his whole heart to serving people with disabilities for almost twenty years. But that's just one of the many miracles of Lourdes. Lourdes speaks to all people who come with open hearts and open minds to help them on their journey to holiness. It tells us what we need, which can sometimes be fairly obvious and other times quite surprising. It also teaches us important lessons, first and foremost how to care for our suffering brothers and sisters. Never have I witnessed people with illness and disability being treated with more respect and reverence than at Lourdes. They are the literal VIPs of the Sanctuary. But Lourdes also shows us that not all sickness and disability is on the outside. And to that end, Lourdes speaks volumes with its messages of peace and healing.

Perhaps you have been one of the millions privileged to make a pilgrimage to Lourdes. I hope then that this book will refresh your memory and rekindle in you Our Lady's call to prayer and conversion. Perhaps you plan to go there—in that case, I hope this book will give you the motivation to do so. Perhaps this book will be the closest you will ever come to experiencing the special grace God still avails through an encounter that happened between His mother and humanity 150 years ago. For you, especially, this book is written. What I've set out to achieve, and hope I have accomplished in the following pages, is an accurate retelling of the story of Bernadette and her apparitions and how, despite the tumultuous times, the Church responded to the Lady's specific request for a chapel and a procession. I also provide a glimpse into the visionary's holy and hidden life after Lourdes, a somewhat lesser-known story, which eventually led to her sanctification. But more than just a historical account, this is a story of the present. It is the story of how Lourdes has become a notable place of pilgrimage for physical, mental, and spiritual healing, attracting the sick and healthy, the poor and rich, believers and nonbelievers alike. It is a shrine so important, the globetrotting Pope John Paul II made it his last place of pilgrimage outside of Italy. Finally, the book looks at how Lourdes, with its Gospel message of prayer, conversion, and sacrifice for the sake of others, fits into the world today and within the mission of the Church to go out and preach the Good News to all the nations.

Our Lady of Lourdes, pray for us.
St. Bernadette, pray for us.

Elizabeth Ficocelli
November 1, 2006
Solemnity of All Saints

PART I
FAITH

1.

BERNADETTE'S EARLY LIFE

On February 11, 1858, in a filthy grotto used as a place to herd and water swine, a young French peasant named Bernadette Soubirous experienced the first of eighteen apparitions of an extraordinarily beautiful Lady dressed in a white gown with a blue sash, with golden roses on each foot. The story has been told many times in many languages, often embellished with romanticized anecdotes, and has been captured for posterity in literature, drama, and art. The attraction to the story of Bernadette and her apparitions is quite understandable, as the tale takes place in the storybook setting of the Pyrenees Mountains on the southern border of France, a rugged natural divider between that country and Spain. The protagonist, Bernadette, is in every sense of the word a simple child, poor and sickly, ignorant in academic matters, but one that possesses a pure and honest faith—a perfect candidate for the mysterious plans of the Divine.

Although the messages imparted by the heavenly visitor at Lourdes were sparse in comparison to other historic apparitions and devoid for the most part of any radical theology or prophetic warnings, belief in the apparitions has endured and flourished, even against tremendous odds. At their start, nineteenth-century France was a nation embroiled in a struggle between its Catholic heritage and the explosion of science and secularism brought about by the French Revolution and its subsequent regimes. Amidst the chaos, the story of the little grotto took root in the hearts of the faithful and came to great fruition despite the opposition of politics, medicine, and, initially, even the clergy.

Today, a century and a half later, Lourdes has become an immensely popular Marian shrine and one of the most visited places of pilgrimage in all Christendom, surpassing even the holy centers of Rome and Jerusalem. Recent annual estimates show that six million pilgrims, both healthy and sick, seek the grotto in the Pyrenees each year. They come for different reasons, from different parts of the globe, and from different walks of life. Together at Lourdes, however, these visitors discover more than just healing waters from which to drink and bathe. They discern in this place a veritable font of faith, hope, and charity that enables them to embrace their life more fully and return to it all the more strengthened. Perhaps even greater than the mystery of the apparitions and the messages—or the cures that are attributed to the healing spring they have produced—this new perspective on life is the greatest miracle of all.

One cannot fully appreciate Bernadette Soubirous without understanding the times and conditions in which she lived. France in the mid-1800s was a country besieged in conflict. Once known as the "eldest daughter of the Church," with Christian roots firmly established as far back as 500 AD, the country was a proud source of popes, great saints, and visionaries. However, France would come to have its entire religious, social, and political identity shaken by the French Revolution of 1789. With this upheaval came the abolishment of Christianity, persecutions of the clergy, and destruction of many churches and monasteries. The Napoleonic Empire, established under Napoleon Bonaparte in 1799, had taken control of the country by force. It boasted an aggressive political agenda with neighboring countries, while the French population engaged in more localized clashes between religion and modernity. Even though Christianity would be restored by the year 1801, there remained a permanent separation of Church and state in French political life.

Geographically, Lourdes was quite distanced from the cosmopolitan centers such as Paris, where many of the debates between religion and secularism were taking place. However, it still felt the pressures of political upheaval and the depressing economic effects that the Industrial Revolution was having on rural areas such as the mountainous region of southern France. Prior to 1866 and the development of the railway, travel to the remote town of Lourdes required a long and arduous coach ride. Another disadvantage was that the town, unlike the mountain villages of Cauterets and Barèges, was not blessed with natural thermal mineral spas. Therefore, it was unable to lure city dwellers to come and "take the waters" while enjoying the clean mountain air.

However, Lourdes was not altogether ill fated. The town was strategically situated at the foothills of the Pyrenees at the intersection of seven different valleys known as the Lavedan, making it a reasonable stopping-point for travelers and pilgrims alike. The steady stream of visitors was an important means for the townspeople to receive news. At Lourdes one could encounter a small percentage of upper class, intellectual, and even noble residents. The town was the seat of the local magistrates and therefore had some government offices. It also had its own newspaper and parish. But the population of Lourdes primarily consisted of millers, quarrymen, shepherds, farmers, forestry workers, and other laborers. It was these ordinary mountain dwellers, with their charming Pyrenean dress, customs, and patois dialect that visitors hoped to experience while taking in the scenery of the surrounding peaks and forests.

Life for Bernadette and her family and neighbors, however, was anything but charming. At the time just prior to the apparitions, Lourdes had a population of about four thousand people, a number that had increased 40 percent since the turn of the century. With this sharp increase in migration came diseases such as cholera and tuberculosis, which were compounded by agricultural shortages and poor nutrition. The times were harsh for the people of the area, and Bernadette's family was no exception. Her father, François Soubirous, was a miller by trade. He married Louise Castérot, the daughter of a master miller. The marriage was one based on love rather than protocol, which was fortunate because genuine affection together with strong faith would enable the couple to endure the difficult trials that awaited them. For a while, however, the years were happy as the Soubirous and extended Castérot families resided and worked together in the Boly Mill. The couple's joy was heightened when their first child, Bernarde Marie (nicknamed Bernadette) entered the world on January 7, 1844. She would be the oldest of nine children, of which only four would survive.

The happy years were not to last for the Soubirous family, however. The introduction of steam mills as a result of the Industrial Revolution put pressure on small family mills, and two seasons of drought that destroyed the corn harvest further compromised business. When François lost an eye in a milling injury, the quality of his flour suffered, which didn't help matters. Finally, the family's generosity toward the poor and their reluctance in extracting money from their impoverished clients sealed their fate—they were forced to move out of the Boly Mill to a cheaper mill.

Things went from bad to worse. Bernadette was struck with cholera in 1855, leaving her frail and sickly with permanent asthma. The family was again forced to move as the local government distributed free flour to offset the famine that had afflicted the area. François tried to "hire out his arms" for wages less than one would pay a horse, but manual labor jobs were few and far between. Louise took in laundry and did some mending, and Bernadette worked for a time as a waitress in her aunt's tavern, but they still could not make ends meet. The family moved from one poor dwelling to another until they had no place left to turn but the street.

A cousin named André Sajous, who was struggling to keep his own family fed, reluctantly offered them a last refuge. The meager hovel was called *Le Cachot,* "the lock-up," or the former town jail. This foreboding place foreshadowed a time when François would serve nine days in the municipal jail after being accused of stealing two sacks of flour. Although he would be acquitted due to lack of evidence, the scandal would leave a permanent blemish on the family, adding shame to their destitution. *Le Cachot* was a dark, damp, and dirty abode, with the entire family crowded into one twelve-by-fourteen-foot room. It was certainly no place for someone as sickly as Bernadette.

A decision was made in September 1857 to send Bernadette to live with her former wet nurse, Marie Laguës, and her family in Batrès, which was about three miles up the mountain from Lourdes. It was hoped that in Batrès Bernadette would find better living conditions and more to eat. The child had been sent to Marie Laguës once before as a baby, after Louise Soubirous was burned by a candle and could no longer nurse her infant. At the time, Marie Laguës had lost her own baby and needed the work as well as the emotional healing of holding an infant in her arms.

From a practical standpoint, sending Bernadette away a second time would also mean one less mouth to feed at the Soubirous home. In exchange, Bernadette would serve the Laguës family as a shepherdess, a housekeeper, and a nanny for their children. Bernadette's family had expected that their eldest daughter would be sent to school at Batrès. However, Marie Laguës had other ideas. The woman decided to teach the child the catechism herself so that Bernadette would be more readily accessible to accomplish her chores. Unfortunately, the poor girl could not read or understand French, as it was quite different from her own local dialect, and the learning was slow and wearisome. In all fairness, Marie Laguës was not the most patient of teachers. It is possible that she still harbored some deep resentment over the fact that Bernadette as a baby had received the milk meant for her deceased firstborn.

After a while, Marie Laguës gave up any attempts at tutoring the ignorant child, claiming that she would never amount to anything. Bernadette responded with tears and silence. Even at this young age, she was developing an ability to accept suffering with patience. "I thought God wanted this," she confided later to her cousin, Jeanne Védère. "When we think, 'God permits this, we don't complain.'"[1] She would have liked to study her catechism with Abbé Ader, the parish priest of Batrès, but she had to tend the sheep on Thursdays when his class was being held. When the priest announced his resignation from the parish in order to pursue a monastic vocation and no replacement was named, Bernadette seized the opportunity. She sent word home that she must return to Lourdes in order to prepare for her First Communion. Meanwhile, the situation at Batrès was worsening, as Marie Laguës lost a third baby and was angry and grieving. Bernadette's only respites from her hard work and the moodiness of her employer were the quiet Thursdays she spent on the grassy slopes with her sheep, amusing herself by building little altars, and the Sundays she walked home to be with her family. On one of these Sundays in January, Bernadette did not return to Batrès until Wednesday. In explanation of her tardiness, the determined girl explained that she had made arrangements with the parish priest in Lourdes to finish her catechesis. She was going home. Little did she know that the one who would truly prepare her for the sacraments would be none other than the Mother of God.

2.

THE APPARITIONS

Bernadette returned from Batrès no better a student than when she had left. Her family enrolled her in the free school of the Sisters of Charity where her catechist, Abbé Pomian, and her younger classmates soon recognized her academic ignorance. The girl made no excuses for herself, accepting her weaknesses and struggling with her work, and still managed a pleasant attitude. The transition from illiterate schoolchild to holy seer would begin on a cold and rainy Thursday, February 11, 1858. That morning, Bernadette noticed the family was out of firewood. The bundle collected the day before had been sold to put bread on the table. Cold and hungry, Bernadette volunteered to help her sister, Toinette, and her friend, Jeanne Abadie, collect firewood, animal bones, rags, and scraps of metal—precious commodities to sell for food and to keep warm in the cold Pyrenean winters. Louise Soubirous consented to let her daughter go on the condition that Bernadette donned a hood and socks due to her asthma.

Collecting firewood was not the easiest of tasks, since the local poor had already scavenged the forests and there were tight restrictions on private property. To avoid any accusations of stealing, the girls headed west from Lourdes toward a remote common ground, Massabielle, meaning "old rock." They decided to walk along the canal of Savy to see where it joined the river Gave de Pau. None of them had ever come this way before. The girls discovered that the two bodies of water converged as the land narrowed to a sandy point directly across from a rocky cliff about thirty feet high. It was the forsaken place of Massabielle, a dark grotto of craggy rock and wild brush. It was an accepted fact among the locals that the area was either haunted or enchanted— or both—and it was generally a place most people chose to avoid. These attitudes were indicative of the Pyrenean people, whose culture blended superstitious beliefs in witches, fairies, forest creatures, magic, and demons along with pious Catholic belief in God and deep devotion to the Holy Virgin.

Toinette and Jeanne removed their shoes and braved the frigid waters of the Savy to reach the other side. Bernadette knew that her mother would not approve of her doing such a thing. She proposed that the girls throw rocks in the water for her to walk across on, or that Jeanne, the larger of the two, carry her across the stream on her back. But the girls were freezing and anxious to complete their task. They could not be slowed by Bernadette and therefore continued down the Gave without her.

Seeing no other way but to cross the canal as the others did, Bernadette sat down to remove her first stocking. At once, she felt a sudden gust of wind. When she looked across the meadow on the other side of the Gave, there was no sign of wind; the leaves of the tall poplar trees remained perfectly still. Bending down to remove her second stocking, she heard the same sound. This time Bernadette looked toward the grotto. About fifteen feet above the ground, she spied a lone wild rosebush growing in a dark niche in the rock with its branches spilling down the cliff. The branches were swaying back and forth as if under some mysterious power. At the same time, she noticed to her astonishment that the niche suddenly brightened, and in the light there appeared a young female figure of exceeding beauty. She wore a long white dress with a blue sash, a long white veil that concealed most of her hair, and a yellow rose on each bare foot. Hanging from her arm was a rosary with large white beads on a golden chain, finished by a large crucifix. Her hands were clasped in prayer.

The figure smiled and beckoned for Bernadette to come closer, but the poor girl was practically frozen with fear and, at the same time, fascination. Instinctively, she began fumbling in the folds of her dress for her rosary, but her arms seemed to fail her. She would write later,

> I put my hand in my pocket, and I found my Rosary there. I wanted to make the Sign of the Cross...I couldn't raise my hand to my forehead. It collapsed on me. Shock got the better of me. My hand was trembling.
>
> The vision made the Sign of the Cross. Then I tried a second time, and I could. As soon as I made the Sign of the Cross, the fearful shock I felt disappeared. I knelt down and I said my Rosary in the presence of the beautiful lady. The vision fingered the beads of her own Rosary, but she did not move her lips. When I finished my Rosary, she signed for me to approach; but I did not dare. Then she disappeared, just like that.[1]

When the apparition was over, everything returned to the way it was. Everything, that is, except Bernadette. Dazed, she removed her second stocking and crossed the little canal, completely oblivious to the cold water. She carefully inspected the hollow of the cave but could find nothing unusual.

When Toinette and Jeanne returned with the firewood, Bernadette asked if they had seen anything. The girls had no idea what she was talking about and were rather perplexed at Bernadette's strange behavior. They were further mystified at how their fragile companion could tolerate the cold water of the stream and could carry a heavy bundle of wood with seemingly little effort. Finally, at Toinette's persistent prompting, Bernadette confided what had happened at the grotto, begging them at the same time not to tell anyone. Her sister was not able to contain herself and told their mother as soon as they arrived home. Louise dismissed the story as nonsense and forbade Bernadette to return to the grotto. After the recent run-in with the police over the stolen bags of flour, she did not want any more trouble with the local authorities.

For the next two days, Bernadette's typical cheerful countenance changed dramatically. She was distressed at the thought of not being able to see the beautiful young Lady again. On Saturday afternoon, she confided her experience and her desire to return to the grotto despite her parents' opposition to Abbé Pomian in the confessional. It was the first time she had made this sacrament. He was curious about her story, particularly her description of the sudden wind, and mentioned it to Abbé Dominique Peyramale, the parish priest. It was received with little interest. By Sunday, February 14, word had spread among Bernadette's classmates at school. This only served to make the child more anxious to return to the grotto. Together she and her sister begged their parents for permission, and finally François and Louise agreed, hoping that another visit to Massabielle would end their daughter's fantasies once and for all.

On this second trip to the grotto, ten children from school accompanied the two sisters. This time the girls decided to take the forest road that rose above Massabielle, and Bernadette was able to descend the steep slope with surprising agility. She was already on her knees at the water's edge praying the Rosary and staring intently at the niche in the wall when the others arrived. The mysterious visitor once again appeared, and this time Bernadette was armed with holy water. She promptly sprinkled it at the apparition until the bottle was empty, but the figure in white merely smiled approvingly. Bernadette then went into a deep trance, during which time the skin on her face tightened and became almost translucent, as if she were glowing from the inside. The expression on her face was one of remarkable peace and beauty. Her intense concentration was unbroken even when latecomer Jeanne, perched high above the grotto, rolled a large rock down the hill as a prank. The sudden noise startled the group that was intently gathered around Bernadette, sending many of the girls screaming and running. Those who stayed to observe Bernadette's unchanged demeanor were truly astonished.

A nearby miller, Antoine Nicolau, was summoned to the grotto. He, too, was struck by Bernadette's countenance and even more amazed at the inexplicable weight of the frail teenager as he gently tried to help the girl to her feet. Despite his endeavors, he was unable to distract her from what she was gazing at so intently, and it was with great effort that he took her to his house to rest until her mother came for her. Louise Soubirous had run all the way from *Le Cachot* to the mill, frightened that her daughter had died based on the descriptions of the frantic witnesses to her behavior. Once Louise arrived at the miller's home and realized that Bernadette was fine, she punished the child severely and put her foot down about any more visits to the grotto. But by now, the whole town was abuzz. Family and friends who knew Bernadette knew it was not in the child's nature to willingly deceive, and they tried to persuade her that what she was experiencing was a dream or an illusion. Others, however, were not so kind, referring to her as a clown and a troublemaker and even striking her in the face.

Two days later, a woman of wealth and position named Madame Milhet summoned Bernadette. She had heard about the apparitions of a Lady in a white dress and blue sash. This description led the woman to speculate that the vision might be the spirit of a recently deceased friend of hers, Élisa Latapie. Élisa had been a holy woman and a member of the Children of Mary, a lay group of women and girls devoted to the Blessed Virgin. Their uniform was a white dress with a blue sash, so Madame Milhet's speculation was natural.

Madame Milhet had provided work for Bernadette's mother in the past and was a woman used to getting her way. She persuaded a reluctant Louise to allow Bernadette to accompany her and her confidante, Antoinette Peyret, to the grotto. They departed in the early morning hours on Thursday, February 18, to attend the first Mass of the day and to avoid attention as they headed to the grotto. The three of them knelt before the niche and Antoinette lit a candle.

The women had brought with them pen and paper and instructed Bernadette to ask the apparition to write down her name, as Bernadette could not read or write herself. When the Lady in white appeared and saw Bernadette with the pen and paper, she glided gently down from the niche into the hollow interior of the cave. When Bernadette came closer, the Lady laughed sweetly, and began to speak for the first time. In the local patois, she told the young seer that it was not necessary to write anything down and asked instead, "Would you have the kindness to come here for fifteen days?" Bernadette was not used to being addressed so formally and politely. She was so taken by the beauty and graciousness of the visitor that she immediately and solemnly promised she would. Before disappearing, the Lady also told Bernadette that she could not promise her happiness in this world, but only in the "other."

After this apparition, Madame Milhet insisted that Bernadette stay at her home, as it was located closer to the grotto. This arrangement did not last long, because Bernadette's aunt and godmother, Aunt Bernarde, did not think it was appropriate and came to bring the youngster home. From the fourth apparition on, Louise Soubirous, Aunt Bernarde, and several other family members started accompanying Bernadette to Massabielle. They encouraged Bernadette to bring a lighted blessed candle to the grotto, a tradition that was quickly emulated by those in attendance, and one that continues to this day. With each visit to Massabielle, the crowds grew larger. At first it was peasant women and children that would gather around Bernadette before the niche, but in time they were joined by men as well as by people of wealth. Many who had come out of curiosity or simply to jest were convinced that the young girl was truly seeing something among the rocks because of her impenetrable tranquility and the transformation of her rather plain features into literal beauty.

It did not take long for the Pyrenean people to conclude that the mysterious visitor to the grotto must be the Holy Virgin, although neither Bernadette nor her supernatural friend had confirmed this fact. Instead Bernadette referred to her beautiful visitor as "Aquerò," the patois word for "that one" or "that thing," giving the connotation of a creature that was not human, but not necessarily divine. This, however, made no difference to the locals. They were certain that the Blessed Mother herself had come to

Massabielle to look favorably upon her poor and suffering children of southern France.

At the fifth apparition on Saturday, February 20, the beautiful Lady taught Bernadette a personal prayer that the seer would never reveal but would pray for the rest of her life. At the end of this visitation, the thirty witnesses to her behavior during the apparition noticed a change in the visionary's face. Normally joyful, radiant, and peaceful during the apparitions, Bernadette grew somber this time when the Lady disappeared. A crowd of one hundred onlookers would notice that her mood was even more remorseful the following day. The child was deeply moved during this apparition, explaining afterward to her family and friends that the Lady had asked her to pray for sinners.

After the sixth apparition, the town fathers, led by Mayor Anselme Lacadé, argued over what should be done about the commotion at Massabielle. Not all of the men were in agreement about whether these events were real, but each had a vested interest in the situation. Lacadé in particular saw a potential marketing opportunity with the arrival of pilgrims to Lourdes. Others were determined not to be caught in a charade. Bernadette was brought in for questioning by the commissioner of police, Monsieur Dominique Jacomet, a tall and imposing man. The girl did not resist. Jacomet had received reports that people were gathering at Massabielle in such great numbers that they were perched precariously on rock ledges and tree limbs. Concerned there might be an accident or an uprising, he was determined to put a stop to the whole matter. He sternly interrogated Bernadette about the apparitions, writing copious notes and then reading them back to her for confirmation. His notes, however, were purposely misconstrued in order to trap the girl in a contradiction. But his efforts were futile, for Bernadette patiently corrected him at every juncture, repeating the answers she had first given with unshakable consistency. She was surprisingly calm and unaffected by the possibility of being thrown into prison if she returned to Massabielle, or by the commissioner's threats to close the grotto. When François Soubirous came to pick up his daughter from the police station, he quietly agreed to keep the girl home. His family was already struggling with being in the spotlight since the apparitions began and he, like his wife, desired to avoid confrontation with the police at all costs.

The following day, Bernadette wrestled with the promise she had made to the Lady in the grotto and the promise her parents had made to the police to keep her from Massabielle. As she was returning to school that afternoon, she felt an irresistible force compelling her to place the apparition's invitation above the opposition of her family and local authorities. She was immediately followed to the grotto by two police officers whose attention was captured by the crowd that had quickly assembled in her wake. When the police demanded to know what she had seen after kneeling in her traditional spot for some time, Bernadette sorrowfully replied, "Nothing." This was the truth, for this time, the mysterious young Lady did not appear. By the time her aunt came to fetch her from the grotto, Bernadette was inconsolable, fearing that she had done something to displease the Lady. Distraught, she confessed a second time to Abbé Pomian about her struggles of obedience. The priest did not reprimand her for returning to the grotto, saying, "They have no right to stop you."[2]

The following day, February 23, the apparition kept its appointment. Bernadette was overjoyed to see *Aqueró,* but her face grew serious again as she stared up at the niche.

Later it was learned that Bernadette had received three secrets from the Lady that she was forbidden to tell anyone since they were meant for her alone. The crowd had grown considerably, and for the first time, gentlemen from the town were present for the apparition. Among them included the first scientist to study Bernadette during her ecstasy, a local physician named Dr. Pierre-Romain Dozous. He came to the grotto with considerable skepticism, but was quickly convinced that something inexplicable was occurring at Massabielle.

Dozous conducted some basic medical tests on Bernadette during her ecstasies and testified that there was nothing abnormal about the girl. "Her pulse was regular, her respiration easy, and nothing indicated any nervous excitement," he reported.[3] Dozous would later serve as an important chronicler of the earliest miracles claimed to occur once the holy fountain was uncovered. Also among the ranks of the elite that day was Jean-Baptiste Estrade, a prominent citizen and local tax collector, who began to keep a detailed account of all he saw and heard regarding Bernadette and the apparitions. His detailed records from firsthand observation and from the input of other witnesses to her ecstasies did much to spread the news and credibility of the apparitions and would provide an invaluable resource for future writers.

On the eighth visitation the proceeding day, in the presence of three hundred people, Bernadette began to move about on her knees during her ecstasy, sometimes crawling on the muddy ground and even stooping down at times to kiss it. *Aqueró* delivered a new message to the child that day: "Penance! Penance! Penance! Pray to God for the conversion of sinners." The sadness in the Lady's face on this day had a profound effect on Bernadette. But it was during the ninth vision on February 25 that the directions from the illuminated visitor became even more telling. For the crowd of 350 gathered that day, it was a moment of excitement and confusion. Bernadette had resumed her posture of walking on her knees as she had the day before. Suddenly, she stood up and began to search for something. The people there were not sure if the apparition was over or not. Intrigued, they watched as Bernadette first headed toward the Gave River and then turned around and entered the cave's interior where she began to crawl around on her hands and knees. She then began to scrape and claw at the reddish clay and stones until a small puddle of muddy water was unearthed. Looking up again toward the niche as if for confirmation, she attempted to fill her hands with this muddy water. It took three attempts until she could obtain more water than earth. On the fourth try she raised the brown liquid to her lips and drank and washed her face with it. Then, to the further disgust of the viewers, she plucked and chewed some of the wild cress growing among the rock. Many were repulsed by this odd behavior and stopped believing on the spot, thinking Bernadette had gone mad.

Aunt Bernarde rushed forward to wipe her goddaughter's mud-streaked face, horrified at this public display. Questioning her all the way home, Bernadette responded calmly that the Lady had told her to drink the water and wash in it, and to kiss the ground as a penance for sinners. By now, Bernadette would do anything for her special friend. Later that afternoon, some of the villagers returned to Massabielle to inspect the spring that Bernadette had uncovered. It was now a slow moving trickle winding its way down to the Gave. People began filling bottles of this water to take home, and it would soon be said to have astonishing effects on the local sick.

That evening, Bernadette was brought in for questioning by the town's imperial prosecutor, Vital Dutour. He got no further than Jacomet in finding the girl either deceitful or insane and was only frustrated at her extraordinary self-assurance. The following day, despite the crowds, the Rosary, and Bernadette's acts of penitence, there was no apparition. Again, the child was crushed. Eight hundred people jostled for a good position for the tenth apparition on February 27, during which Bernadette again drank of the spring and did her usual acts of penance. Over eleven hundred people would be on the scene for the eleventh visitation on February 28, tightly wedged between the sheer cliff of Massabielle and the Gave. This time the seer was interrogated afterward by the examining magistrate, Judge Clément Ribes. He, like his predecessors, was ineffective in keeping Bernadette from her appointments in the grotto.

On March 1, the date of the twelfth apparition, there was a clergy member for the first time among the throng of fifteen hundred. He was Abbé Antoine Dézirat, a newly ordained priest from the neighboring town of Omex, who did not know that clergy were forbidden to go to the grotto. Having the opportunity to be in close proximity to the visionary during her ecstasy, he commented later, "What struck me was the joy, the sadness reflected in Bernadette's face....Respect, silence, recollection reigned everywhere. Oh, it was good to be there. It was like being at the gates of paradise."[4]

It was on this same day that the first authenticated cure took place at the spring. By now the slow trickle of the underground fountain had become a steady stream that the locals had pooled with clumps of turf. One of the witnesses to Bernadette during the apparitions was a thirty-nine-year-old resident of the nearby town of Loubajac named

Catherine Latapie. Eighteen months earlier, the woman had fallen out of a tree in an attempt to obtain acorns for her hog. The fall caused her to dislocate her arm, causing nerve damage in the shoulder and paralysis of some of her fingers. During the night between February 28 and March 1, Catherine was moved by a sudden impulse to rise at 3:00 in the morning, wake her young children, and set off for Lourdes. At the time she was at the end of her third pregnancy. Arriving at the grotto at dawn, she met Bernadette and knelt down to pray. Then, seeking relief from her pain and immobility, Catherine plunged her useless hand into the icy mountain water. Instantly her fingers became mobile. It is said that after the submersion, she immediately went into labor and rushed home to deliver a healthy baby boy, Jean-Baptiste, who would grow up to be a priest.

News of this healing only increased the crowds and the excitement at the grotto the next day. On March 2, during the thirteenth apparition in the presence of an estimated 1,650 people, Bernadette was given an important directive by *Aqueró*. She was told to tell the priests that the Lady desired a chapel to be built at Massabielle and that she wanted the people to come there in procession. Abbé Pomian sent Bernadette directly to Abbé Peyramale, the parish priest, with this news. Peyramale was well informed by now about the excited crowds at the grotto and the stories in the newspapers alleging that the Holy Virgin was appearing in Massabielle, although Bernadette had never made this claim herself. Despite the recent increase the pastor was seeing in Mass attendance and confessions, he had a reserved attitude about the whole matter. He was less than hospitable when Bernadette, accompanied by two of her aunts, showed up at the rectory. At the first mention of a processional, Peyramale launched into a tirade that sent the three visitors scurrying. Bernadette was so frightened that she forgot all about delivering the second part of the message for a chapel to be built at Massabielle. Soliciting the help of another relative, she returned that evening to the rectory and finished conveying her message in the presence of Peyramale and three other priests. While she departed joyfully at having completed her mission, she left behind four very troubled clergymen.

By now, the news of apparitions and miracles at Massabielle had reached Paris and other cities of France. No longer were the crowds gathered at the grotto in prayer limited to the inhabitants of Lourdes. People were pouring in from all over France and beyond. Three thousand anxious onlookers crowded into the grotto around Bernadette and in the areas across the Gave and Savy for her fourteenth anticipated apparition, but none came that morning. It would not be until later that day, in the presence of only about one hundred people, that Bernadette would return to the grotto and see the Lady. When she reported Abbé Peyramale's negative response, the Lady only smiled and repeated her desires. The visionary had no choice but to approach the parish priest a second time. This time Peyramale demanded to know the identity of the Lady who was asking for a chapel and a procession. Furthermore, he requested a sign—that the wild rosebush growing in the oval niche where the Lady appeared would burst into bloom despite the fact that it was winter and the bush was quite barren. Bernadette promised she would relay his requests. Inwardly, Peyramale was impressed with the girl's courage and persistence, but the talk of apparitions continued to disturb him.

It was widely acknowledged that the following day, Thursday, March 4, marked the end of the fifteen days, or fortnight, that the beautiful Lady had requested of Bernadette.

Surely this would be the day that the rosebush would bloom and the identity of the mysterious young Lady would be revealed once and for all. The police were on hand to assure the safety of ten thousand hopeful spectators, all trying to squeeze in and around the area. On that much-anticipated day, an apparition did occur of about forty-five minutes, but there was no miracle of the rosebush and no message for the anxious onlookers. The crowd left, disappointed. Abbé Peyramale was not satisfied either. Although the newspapers took advantage of the uneventful conclusion to the fortnight, Bernadette had peace in her heart. True, she had not succeeded in learning the Lady's name or understanding exactly why she had been asked to come for fifteen days, but she was pleased to have met the Lady and delivered her message. There was no longer an attraction to go to the grotto.

Three weeks later, however, on the eve of March 25, the feast of the Annunciation, Bernadette awoke from her sleep with the familiar and joyful anticipation of seeing the Lady again. At the first sign of day, she and her parents returned to the grotto to find many others gathered for this special feast day. Even the excitement of seeing the beautiful Lady once again did not deter Bernadette from trying to acquire her name. In her ecstasy she pleaded with the beautiful Lady to reveal who she was—not once, but four times, wringing her hands in despair. *Aqueró* smiled in silence. Finally, she stopped smiling. She slipped her rosary over her right arm, unfolded her hands, and extended them to the ground. Then, folding her hands at her breast, she raised her eyes to heaven and proclaimed solemnly, "I am the Immaculate Conception."

These words were obscure and difficult for Bernadette, but she was filled with gratitude that her request was at last answered. She placed her candle in the rocks in thanksgiving and hurried off to see Abbé Peyramale. Not understanding the great revelation that had just occurred, she repeated the name to herself over and over to make sure that the words would be conveyed properly. Her uncle stopped her along the way and pressed her about her obvious joy. Bernadette whispered the words she had heard to her uncle and hurried on. She must tell Abbé Peyramale. Flinging open the door to the rectory, she triumphantly pronounced the long-awaited answer: "I am the Immaculate Conception!"

The parish priest was utterly dumbfounded by this proclamation. Mary's sinlessness was a subject that had been long debated by theologians and long held true by the faithful. At the Council of Trent three centuries earlier, Mary's sinlessness was decreed an article of faith, making it an optional belief. But, Peyramale recalled, Pope Pius IX had just settled matters once and for all four years prior by proclaiming the Immaculate Conception official church dogma. Citing scripture, liturgy, reason, precedent, and tradition, the teaching essentially declared that only a perfect vessel would be fitting to hold perfection itself. Therefore, Mary *had* to be conceived free from original sin in order to fulfill her mission of bringing the Son of God into the world. Through grace, she was, in essence, redeemed by Jesus even before her conception. By using these specific words, "I am the Immaculate Conception," the Lady in the grotto accomplished three things: She affirmed the new dogma, she acknowledged her heavenly identity, and she legitimated Bernadette's visions.

Peyramale knew there was no practical way that an illiterate peasant of the Pyrenees would be familiar with such a theological phrase. Recognizing the seriousness of the matter and still at a loss for words, he sent Bernadette home. When Abbé Pomian seemed equally stupefied by her report, Bernadette left confused and disappointed. Had she misunderstood the Lady's name? Why were the priests acting this way? It would not be until later that day that she would have her answer from Monsieur Estrade and realize to her amazement that the beautiful Lady in the grotto was truly the Holy Virgin after all.

This news set off a new wave of excitement among the people, who promptly erected a little altar. These actions drew considerable concern from local officials and clergy alike. Peyramale notified the bishop of Tarbes, Monsignor Bertrand-Sévère Laurence, who chose to remain cautiously neutral regarding the apparitions. Displeased with his inaction, the mayor and the public commissioner of Lourdes contacted the prefect of Tarbes, Baron Oscar Massy. The prefect was not excited about the surge of devotion stemming from Lourdes. In his opinion, it was superstitious and old-fashioned and would only increase the animosity between the Church and the government. Massy immediately ordered that Bernadette be examined by three responsible doctors. After intense questioning and testing, to which Bernadette submitted patiently, these handpicked experts concluded that she was of sound mind and body. Still, the prefect gave orders to dismantle the rustic altar, stripping it of the candles, rosaries, flowers, and other small gifts that had been left by the pilgrims, and to close down the grotto to the public. He was not willing to take chances with what he deemed religious hysteria.

The removal of the religious items and makeshift altar inflamed the local poor, causing them to unite and defy orders to stay away from the grotto. Meanwhile, attention on Bernadette and her family was becoming fever-pitched.

People flocked to *Le Cachot* day and night to seek the visionary for her prayers or advice, or to present her family with all sorts of gifts. Despite the Soubirous's dire state of poverty, these gifts were all politely but firmly refused. Bernadette understood that it was not right to accept them. She did not see herself as anything special and could not comprehend the growing interest in her. She had also come to understand through her apparitions that there was a greater state of poverty than that which her family suffered: the poverty of sin and disbelief. Recognizing that her impoverished lifestyle was a form of penance, she did not desire to change it. Her resistance to the temptations of money and fame and the embrace of her poverty would later be considered an authentic witness to the reality of the apparitions.

Stories ran rampant that the young seer had supernatural abilities, such as being unharmed when her hand rested for a while on the flame of her candle during her seventeenth vision on April 7, an incident that was witnessed by Dr. Dozous. She was also credited with the cure of a blind girl whom she hugged after one of her visions at the grotto, and for the improvement of a young boy who had a strange illness in which he could not close his mouth. Bernadette purposely maintained a low profile about the subject of miraculous reports. The Lady had not told her that the underground spring would produce cures or that she was now privileged with any supernatural abilities. In fact, Bernadette did not seek a cure for her own illness at the spring she had unearthed at Massabielle. Instead, she traveled to the neighboring town of Cauterets to relieve her asthma symptoms in their thermal spa waters. When questioned, the visionary insisted with genuine humility that if there were miracles taking place at Lourdes, it had nothing

to do with her; it could only be due to the intercession of
the Blessed Virgin Mary. It wasn't long before other people
began reporting visions of the Holy Virgin, although none
of these claims could be substantiated. The temporary distraction from attention on Bernadette enabled the girl to try
and regain some normalcy to her life by continuing her
studies, which seemed no less of a struggle. She finally
made her First Holy Communion on June 3, under the spiritual direction of Abbé Pomian. Reception of this sacrament
was a great consolation for the fourteen-year-old in the face
of all the publicity and pressures she was experiencing.
These anxieties only heightened as police officially barricaded the entrance to Massabielle on June 15, with the
reluctant consent of the bishop. Although frequent
Communion was not the custom in those days, Bernadette
sought opportunities to receive the Holy Eucharist whenever possible. One such occasion was the feast of Our Lady
of Mount Carmel on July 16. The peace that the young girl
experienced from receiving Holy Communion stayed with
her the entire day, and as evening approached, she felt com-
pelled again to gaze upon her beloved grotto, knowing she
could not enter it now due to the barricades.

Accompanied by one of her aunts, the two headed to
Massabielle from the other side of the Gave, where they
could see the stone formation from across the river. There
were small groups of women already assembled and kneeling in prayer. Within moments, Bernadette's face became
joyful and illuminated. After her ecstasy, she explained to
those gathered that she had seen the Lady, just as before,
and never had she looked more beautiful. There had been
no exchange of words. When the women asked how the
child could see the Lady from such a distance, she
responded, "I saw neither the boards nor the Gave; it

seemed to me I was at the grotto, no farther away than at the other times. I saw nothing but the Blessed Virgin."[5] This ability to see beyond difficulties and focus on what was important would be an insight that would strengthen Bernadette the rest of her life. And so the apparitions ended as they began, in beauty and in silence. Quietly, inconspicuously, the heavenly visits at Massabielle were over.

3.

THE CHURCH'S RESPONSE

Bernadette Soubirous was by no means the first person in her country to report an apparition of the Virgin Mary. Nineteenth-century France was the scene of repeated appearances of the Blessed Mother with great proclamations, despite—or perhaps due to—the turbulence of the times. Just twelve years prior to the apparitions at Lourdes, two peasant children named Melanie Calvat, age fifteen, and Maximin Girard, age eleven, experienced a series of apparitions of a Sorrowful Virgin that occurred while they were tending sheep outside their village of La Salette in the French Alps. The messages imparted to the children contained serious warnings about future events for the world, including the predictions of war involving France, Italy, Spain, and England. Approved by the Church in 1851, La Salette quickly became known as a place for miracles and pilgrimage.

Sixteen years prior to that, in 1830, an event of even greater notoriety occurred, this time in a far more metropolitan setting: on the rue du Bac in the heart of Paris. Here, a twenty-four-year-old novice of the Daughters of Charity of St. Vincent de Paul named Catherine Labouré received three apparitions of the Madonna at the motherhouse of her order. Once again, the messages foretold of great trials and tribulations that would befall people if they did not mend their ways and turn back to God. Unique to her apparitions, Labouré was shown a spectacular image of the Blessed Mother holding a globe in her hands. The globe disappeared, leaving the Virgin's hands covered with rings set with precious stones from which emanated brilliant rays of light toward the ground, revealing a white globe under her feet. An oval frame surrounded this extraordinary image with the words, "O Mary, conceived without sin, pray for us who have recourse to thee." Labouré was instructed to have a medal struck of this image with a promise that whoever wore it would receive great graces. Achieved two years later in 1832, the medal became known as the Miraculous Medal and was worn first on the blue sashes of the Children of Mary and later around the necks of millions of the faithful, many of whom continue to report miracles due to its wearing.

Even the Pyrenees region where Bernadette lived had its own history of visitations. It was not uncommon for statues to be erected in or around the numerous caves in the mountains, marking the places where the Holy Virgin was believed to have appeared to seers, often shepherd children. However, there were many other claims of apparitions through the years that could not be authenticated, and in that light (and in consideration of the volatile times), local church representatives had to proceed with caution when it came to the events at Lourdes.

Monsignor Bertrand-Sévère Laurence, the bishop of nearby Tarbes, which included Lourdes as part of its diocesan territory, demonstrated typically cautious feelings about the apparitions at Massabielle, yet he refused to make a hasty decision on the matter. He was a practical, open-minded man, a peasant by birth, who could well relate to the plight of his people. Like them, Laurence had a strong devotion to the Holy Virgin, and he sought her intercession to achieve his main focus: to rebuild the Church after the effects of the revolution and to incorporate Lourdes into mainstream French Catholicism. The bishop believed that the new government of Louis Napoleon's Second Empire would be good for the Church and that authentic apparitions were a blessing to the nation. As early as April 11, he had submitted his opinion on the apparitions to the prefect, Baron Oscar Massy, the region's highest civil authority and a long-time personal friend: "The doctors rule out fraud; that's something; they allow that hallucinations and ecstasy might follow from a cerebral lesion. It's possible—very possible; it's even very likely. For myself, I admit the value of their approach. I only want to add that I believe the supernatural is possible, although in the present case I await further proof of it."[1]

For perhaps the first time, Prefect Massy did not share the bishop's point of view. The subject of the apparitions at Lourdes would eventually cause a severing of their long-term alliance, as Massy remained committed to distinguishing between true Catholic religion and what he felt was dangerous superstition. His order to close down Massabielle was increasingly difficult to enforce by local police because of the sheer number of pilgrims determined to cross the barriers to the grotto. Many were foreign, wealthy, or prestigious—or even members of the clergy or religious—which made their arrest downright impractical. Massy's authority was further challenged when Bishop Laurence appointed the Episcopal Commission of Inquiry in July to formally begin investigating the apparitions, demonstrating the seriousness of his intent. In the end, Massy would lose not only the battle of the grotto but his seat as prefect when he was transferred to another post.

Of the many visitors to the grotto that July, there were two that were particularly influential in changing the perception of Lourdes from a local phenomenon to one of national interest. The first was Louis Veuillot, a powerful and radically conservative Catholic convert and journalist. Despite his poor upbringing, Veuillot was able to use his writing skills to eventually find a secure position within Parisian journalism. He was inspired to join the Church after a trip to Rome, and in the wake of his conversion he wrote numerous sharp-tongued articles debating free-thinkers, philosophers, and other learned individuals on the subject of religion versus secularism. When the journalist came to Lourdes, he was at the height of his popularity. His impression of the faithful and of the visionary herself was quite favorable, and writing about what he had experienced at Lourdes did much to publicize the apparitions in the grotto.

The other visitor of extreme importance was Amirale Bruat, governess of the prince imperial. While Emperor Louis Napoleon (Napoleon III) himself did not have much interest in religion, his wife, Empress Eugenie, had a solid Catholic devotion. It was this beautiful Spanish aristocrat who sent the governess to the grotto to fetch water from the miraculous spring at Lourdes to improve the health of her two-year-old son and heir to the throne of France. Bruat traveled ninety miles, escorted to Lourdes by her three daughters and a nun, and was recognized immediately as a lady of great importance both by her attire and her entourage. Abbé Pomian, who felt that the governess's visit to Massabielle was providential, personally welcomed her. Evidently, the water must have proven beneficial to Empress Eugenie's son, because three months later orders were issued by Napoleon III to allow free access to the grotto.

Although the famous apparitions of Lourdes had come to an end, focus on Bernadette was far from over. Both vis-

itors to Lourdes and locals alike sought to touch the peasant girl and seek her blessing on their holy objects. She constantly shrank from such attention. While the questions
were unending, the answers and descriptions Bernadette
provided were remarkably consistent. She neither embellished nor omitted details and did her best to answer the
same (and often trivial) questions over and over, although it
was physically and mentally fatiguing. Abbé Peyramale had
long overcome his own personal doubts about the visions
and had appointed himself as the girl's spiritual protector.
He was careful not to spoil her, but to maintain her sincerity and humility, and therefore it was not uncommon for
him to admonish her in the presence of others.

Louise and François Soubirous were scrupulous about
refusing gifts of money or food from the steady stream of
their daughter's admirers. But they were not totally immune
to blessing. The apparitions healed them of being complete
outcasts in society, and work opportunities began to return.
By September, the Soubirous family was able to move out of
Le Cachot and into a rented room at the home of a distant
relative, Jean DeLuc, a baker and café owner. Some months
later, François was able to resume his position as a miller
and rented the Gras Mill. Wherever they moved, however,
the crowds followed them. Bernadette worked with an
unpaid tutor to continue her schooling. She also served as a
babysitter and helped around the mill when endless visitors
did not interrupt her. When she could, the young girl
would go to the grotto and pray. Finally, concerned for her
health under the intensity of growing public interest,
Peyramale made arrangements in July 1860 for Bernadette
to live and work at the local hospice with the Sisters of
Nevers. Shortly after, he and the mayor helped the Soubirous

family move into the Lacade Mill, a more appropriate environment for the family.

In the somewhat protected environment of the hospice, Bernadette happily performed menial chores. Her greatest joy was working with the younger children at the school, as it reminded her of home. She also enjoyed caring for the poor and tending the sick in the infirmary, which she did with a genuine nurturing ability. The sisters were more successful in teaching Bernadette how to speak, read, and write in French. This enabled the young visionary to document for the first time her own simple account of what had happened at Massabielle. But even in the confines of the hospice, Bernadette was still called upon regularly to relate the story in person to a long list of people that Abbé Peyramale would send her way. Being "shown off" in this manner was a great penance for the visionary.

In the meantime, the Episcopal Commission of Inquiry established by Bishop Laurence to investigate the apparitions was busy interrogating not only Bernadette but her family and friends, eyewitnesses of her ecstasies in the grotto, and recipients of so-called miraculous cures. It would take a total of four years of intense investigation—including the determination of seven cases of inexplicable healings due to contact with the waters of the spring—for the commission to formally approve the apparitions at Massabielle. The decision was based on conformity of the apparitions to the Gospel message, the authenticity of the life of the seer, and the fruits of holiness that flowed on the people of God. The much-anticipated news was finally announced on January 18, 1862: "We hold that the Immaculate Mary, Mother of God, actually appeared to Bernadette Soubirous on the eleventh of February, 1858, and on the days following, to the number of eighteen times, in the grotto of Massabielle, near the town of Lourdes; that this apparition bears all the signs of authenticity and that the faithful are free to consider it true."[2]

Bishop Laurence had the fortunate insight to purchase the reverenced grotto and its surrounding area from the city of Lourdes in 1861, a full year before his commission rendered their final verdict. Once the apparitions received official Church approval, Peyramale and Laurence worked together on plans to beautify the grotto and improve public access to it, which required leveling much of its rugged hilliness. They also moved ahead with plans to accommodate the Virgin's request for a chapel, which they envisioned as a large structure or crypt built into the rock rising over the grotto, with a church above it. Meanwhile, the renowned sculptor Joseph Fabisch was contracted to create a marble likeness of the Madonna for the oval niche. Fabisch had interviewed Bernadette before he started his work and showed her photos of an early model of the statue. When the finished product was brought to her for her approval, she could not hide her disappointment. It was beautiful, but the sculpted figure was much older and larger in size than the illuminated young Lady she had seen in her apparitions.

Bernadette would never find true consolation in any artistic rendition of the Virgin, for according to the seer, the magnificent young Lady was far too beautiful to capture in mere human ways. Nonetheless, the statue was enshrined with great ceremony on April 4, 1864, with ten thousand pilgrims taking part in the first official procession to the grotto. With its white dress, blue sash, and golden roses on each foot, it would become the image for Our Lady of Lourdes. Abbé Peyramale thought it best that Bernadette did not attend the procession due to her poor health and also to preserve her humility. She obeyed, sharing with her cousin, "I'm as happy to stay in bed as I would be to go to the grotto. I would like to go....God does not want me to. His will be done....Don't feel sorry for me; when we do what God wants, no one should feel sorry."[3]

Celebrated architect Hippolyte Duran, a convert, was commissioned to work on sketches for the lower and upper levels of a magnificent Gothic structure befitting the visit of the Holy Virgin to the Pyrenees. At the same time, there was massive engineering to the grotto and surrounding area. François Soubirous was among the team of quarry workers excavating the foundation for the building. Much of the wilderness had been cleared away, and concrete was poured over the natural ground at Massabielle, even over the Savy millstream, which was piped underground to the Gave. To prohibit pilgrims from entering the interior cave of the grotto or from climbing the cliff face in an attempt to seek a souvenir (the wild rosebush had already been plucked clean weeks after the apparitions began), a wrought-iron grill was installed in 1864. In a way, these renovations foreshadowed Bernadette's impending preservation at the motherhouse of the Sisters of Nevers.

Due to the limited space in the area along the Gave, Duran's massive sanctuary needed to be constructed on a hill twenty-four meters above the river, which required even greater feats of engineering. The project had a difficult start, with designers and foremen arguing among themselves, resulting in a delay of nearly two years. Troubles continued in keeping the enormous project within budget. Abbé Peyramale had a vested interest in this new church, anticipating that it would become his new parish. This would not be the case. In 1866, Bishop Laurence invited the Missionaries of the Immaculate Conception from Garaison to move to Lourdes, as these men were experienced in promoting and protecting shrines in the Diocese of Tarbes.

The arrival of the Garaison Fathers would mark a formal separation of "the Domain"—the grotto and its surrounding area—and the town parish. Peyramale and the new shrine priests did not see eye-to-eye on a number of matters. With the completion of the crypt of the basilica in 1866, processionals originating at the old parish diminished. Frustrated, Peyramale initiated construction of a new and grand parish in the old section of Lourdes, but he would die before it could be completed. The building would stand roofless and incomplete for fifteen years until some of Peyramale's supporters could raise the necessary funds to complete it some twenty-five years later.

The year 1866 was a significant one for Lourdes. In addition to the arrival of the Garaison Fathers and the completion of the crypt, the long-awaited railway had finally rolled into town, connecting the emerging shrine to the rest of Europe and the world. The crypt was dedicated that same year with great pomp and circumstance, including a celebration of the first Mass. A special visitor was in attendance that day: Bernadette Soubirous. She was concealed in the white dress and blue sash of the Children of Mary in order to protect her identity from the exuberant and adoring crowd. The sermon delivered that day praised Bishop Laurence and Abbé Peyramale but made no mention of the Pyrenean visionary. A small unnoticed figure in the vast crowd, Bernadette took in all the wonder, clearly understanding that neither she nor the grotto would ever be the same; they were changed forever due to eighteen visits from the Mother of God.

It was normal protocol for a visionary in those days to enter the religious life, and by now Bernadette's heart was prepared for a cloistered and contemplative lifestyle such as that of the Carmelites, where she could retreat even further from public view. She was particularly attracted to the order's strict lifestyle of vigils, fasting, discipline, and mortification. Her body, unfortunately, was not as well prepared as her heart, and it would not allow her to comply with the demanding rule of the Carmelites. Her attention, therefore, was directed toward an active life of serving the poor and the sick. A number of teaching and nursing orders sought her, eager for the opportunity to have a visionary among their ranks. In the end, however, Bernadette accepted the invitation of the bishop of Nevers to join the order of those with whom she had worked at the hospice for so many years.

In contrast to the fervor of the development of the grotto, the chapel, and the processions, Bernadette quietly entered the motherhouse of the Sisters of Nevers, halfway across France and some three hundred miles from home. Leaving her beloved grotto and the only home and family she had ever known was the greatest sacrifice of her life, but she had come to accept the fact that her mission at Lourdes was finished. After all, "Lourdes was not heaven."[4] The younger sisters at Nevers were excited about Bernadette's entrance to their convent, but some of the older ones were concerned that a celebrated visionary could have the virtue of humility required of a religious. This proved to be an unnecessary worry, for Bernadette quickly demonstrated herself as quite humble and content in her new private life. She was ordered to tell her story only once, to the entire congregation, and then was forbidden to speak about the subject any further. This could not suit her any better. From that point on, the sisters were careful to show her no special attention. The superior general, Mère Josephine Imbert, and the mistress of novices, Mère Marie-Thérèse Vauzou, even went out of their way to ensure her humility, a behavior encouraged by Abbé Peyramale.

The relationship between Bernadette and her novice mistress was a complex one from the beginning. The fundamental problem for Mère Vauzou was trying to find a place within the ordinary religious life for an extraordinary individual. She had to continually guard herself against the danger of potentially reverencing the seer. This tension would increase over time, particularly as Mère Vauzou rose to superior general. There are several speculations for the difficulties between the two women. In those days, superiors used withdrawal of affection to break novices of their self-will in order to form them in obedience. However, some maternal presence was necessary to help young novices adjust to their new surroundings. While other young sisters opened themselves up to their novice mistress, Bernadette remained evasive and secretive, which irritated Mère Vauzou. It was not the visionary's intention to hurt her novice mistress; she was being led interiorly to a new kind of sanctity based on the Gospels, one without works or words, a way hidden from the wise and the learned. Another problem was that Mère Vauzou did not share the same devotion to the Holy Virgin. She instead preferred a Christ-centered faith grounded in devotion to the Sacred Heart. A third problem was that she could never quite accept that someone as simple and unimpressive as Bernadette would be chosen for such an important mission.

Three weeks after her arrival at Nevers, Bernadette received the habit and the religious name Sister Marie-Bernard. The young nun was obedient and patient, demonstrating a skill for sewing and for working with the novices. Their feelings of homesickness and loneliness were quite understandable to her. She was friendly to everyone and maintained a delightful sense of humor, but she was serious when it came to prayer and the Eucharist. To develop her virtue she accepted correction easily and preferred the lowliest duties. She quickly earned many confidantes at the motherhouse, to whom she gave solid spiritual direction. In sum, Bernadette was well liked by all.

Her poor health continued to be an issue, however, nearly claiming her life that autumn and prompting an early profession of vows. (It would be the first of four times that Bernadette would receive last rites due to her close encounters with death.) However, the young novice recovered to renew her formal vows of profession the following year in the presence of the entire community, becoming an official member of the Congregation of Sisters of Charity and Christian Instruction. Unlike the other newly professed sisters, Bernadette was not given an assignment by the bishop. It was felt that she would be better protected from the public at the motherhouse than at a remote hospital or school, but the reason given to Bernadette in order to maintain her humility was that she did not have the skills of her professed sisters. Therefore, she remained at the motherhouse for the next eight years, where she patiently and kindly cared for the infirm sisters when she wasn't spending time in the infirmary herself.

The order to which Bernadette belonged called its members to a life of contemplation and active service. As much as she desired these, both charisms presented an obstacle for the young nun. She was not gifted with the ability to memorize long prayers or to read volumes of works, and she often confessed to having trouble with meditation. On the other hand, as much as she longed for the opportunity to serve others, her physical stamina was always a consideration. Eventually, Bernadette would become complacent with the one thing she could do well, and that was to suffer.

For Bernadette, suffering had begun long before her years in the convent or in the hospice. It had begun with a

childhood battle to survive dire poverty. With the apparitions came additional suffering. The visionary was made to
endure harassment by police and authorities, criticism and
disbelief of friends and neighbors, intrusiveness of prying
visitors, and tendencies for others to flatter, bribe, or venerate her. In the hospice and the convent, Bernadette's suffering continued in her feelings of being useless and inactive.
In addition, far from home, she would grieve the deaths of
her mother, father, and Abbé Peyramale. To look upon photos of her changed grotto and hometown caused her great
sorrow, and more than once she had to write letters admon-
ishing family members for profiting from the sale of sou-
venirs at the shrine. (As the eldest of the Soubirous
children, Bernadette was still expected to oversee sibling
quarrels and other matters, despite the miles between her
and her family.) Finally, there were still a number of inquis-
itive visitors to the motherhouse, including counts, bishops,
and journalists who wanted to question Bernadette about
the apparitions, even as she lay in the infirmary. But by now,
between time and distance and ill health, Bernadette's memory was starting to fade, particularly regarding dates, and
she became concerned that she might make errors about
what had happened—yet another suffering. She frequently
had to answer in humility and honestly, "I don't remember."

When Bernadette's failing health required a less rigor-
ous position than the infirmary, she was assigned as sacristan to the chapel. She loved to spend this additional time
in the presence of the Blessed Sacrament, but it came with
a penance. Once again she was subjected to a public hopeful for a glimpse of the world-famous visionary. Although
they did not know it was Bernadette herself who politely
told them that Sister Marie-Bernard was unable to come to
the chapel, it was still emotionally trying for her. She liked

to withdraw into the headpiece of her habit for privacy, much like she used to do with the hood on her cape at the time of the apparitions. Her role as sacristan did not last long; the tuberculosis that was most likely contracted early in her life was now at an advanced stage, and Sister Marie-Bernard was sent to retire to the infirmary in which she had served so many others. She would quip to her sisters that she now had the full-time job of being sick.

In the meantime, back at Lourdes, the Church's response to the Virgin's request for a chapel was answered. It was an impressive structure that loomed above the grotto, completed in 1872 and officially named the Basilica of the Immaculate Conception in 1874. Crowned with a tall distinctive spire and bell tower, some seventy meters in height, it could be seen throughout the surrounding valley, marking its Catholic approval on the apparitions and pointing the way to pilgrimage, penitence, and redemption. The interior of the church was visually arresting as well, decorated with intricate carvings and stained-glass windows depicting key Marian events, including the Annunciation, Visitation, Assumption, Coronation, and of course, the apparitions at Lourdes. The main altar was strategically placed directly above the place where the Lady appeared in the grotto.

The celebrations at Lourdes in July 1876 for the consecration of the basilica and the coronation of a new grand statue of the Madonna attracted one hundred thousand pilgrims and a fresh wave of visitors to Nevers to see the ailing visionary. Many had invited Bernadette to come to Lourdes for the celebrations. She refused, explaining to a sister, "If I could transport myself down to the grotto in a balloon and pray for a few moments when there was no one there, I'd gladly go; but if I have to travel like everyone else and find myself in the middle of the crowd, I'd rather stay here."[5]

No sooner had the cathedral been completed than it became evident it would not be big enough to accommodate the ever growing number of pilgrims. Work then commenced on an adjoining church, the Basilica of the Rosary. Featuring a Romano-Byzantine style architecture designed by architect Leopold Hardy, it incorporated colossal ramps up and around the structure, symbolizing the arms of the Church opened wide to welcome its multitude of international visitors. The ramps encircled a large plaza called Rosary Square that connected to a grand esplanade the length of eleven football fields, a perfect size for hundreds of thousands of pilgrims to process.

Between the construction of the basilicas and the advent of the railway, Lourdes underwent a process of significant urbanization. Major roadways were built to accommodate increasing traffic, necessitating the demolition of older sections of the town and causing the loss of some of the town's original character. The Garaison Fathers arranged a new highway, *Boulevard de la Grotte*, which connected the railway station directly to the Domain, bypassing the town of Lourdes altogether. The influx of pilgrims and new inhabitants to the area created a boom in the building of hotels, restaurants, and other shops and businesses around the grotto. As a result, Lourdes became divided into two towns—the original old town or high town, and the new town or low town built around the Sanctuary. Twenty years after the apparitions, the once sleepy mountain town of Lourdes was barely recognizable.

The same could be said for the dying visionary herself, whose features had been changed not only by age, but from the physical ravages of cholera, asthma, and tuberculosis as well as the emotional trials of being scrutinized, disciplined, and humiliated. Bernadette spent her last four months in agony on one of the small simple beds draped with curtains that she referred to as her "white chapel." Her physical anguish included suffocating asthma and chest pains, fits of coughing up blood, a painful tumor on her knee and other bone decay that made it impossible to move without pain or even to sleep, as well as abscesses in her ears that resulted in partial deafness. Her wasted body was covered with raw bedsores. Perhaps recalling her childhood, she confided to one of the sisters, "I have been ground in the mill like a grain of wheat."[6] In the last weeks, as if the physical suffering was not enough, God seemed to remain hidden and silent as the dying nun's mind was filled with doubts and temptations. Although she did not talk much about it, it seemed by every indication that she was truly suffering a dark night of the soul as described by St. John of the Cross. With each passing day, she suffered what she referred to as her passion, taking consolation in the end only in the crucifix. When her strength gave out and she could no longer hold it in her hands, the sisters fastened it to her. In imitation of Christ's passion, her last request was for a small drink of water. Then, on April 16, 1879, at 3:15 p.m., Bernadette Soubirous left this world for happiness in the "other," issuing a final prayer, "Holy Mary, Mother of God, pray for me, a poor sinner...."[7]

Bernadette's devoted fans would not witness the reality of the visionary's increasing age and sickliness leading up to her death at the age of thirty-five, thirteen years after her entrance into the convent. Their image of the seer as a fourteen-year-old Pyrenean girl would be forever etched in their minds. This was completely understandable. For one, cholera and poor nutrition had stunted Bernadette's growth. She never grew taller than a childlike stature of four feet, six inches. But more importantly, a number of professional photographs that were taken both at the hospice and at the motherhouse perpetuated the image of Bernadette, child visionary. Quite conscious that Bernadette was a likely candidate for future sainthood, Abbé Peyramale and others had a keen interest in preserving the visionary's purity and humility. Professional photographers staged photos of the young woman dressed in thick layers of Pyrenean costume to hide her developing womanhood. She was required to remain in awkward positions for long periods of time while the photographers made stilted attempts to recreate her ecstasy in the grotto. Like the freshly paved Massabielle, Bernadette the child visionary was being carefully preserved for all time through the new technology of black and white photography.

When it was announced to the world that Bernadette Soubirous had expired, multitudes came to the chapel at Nevers to venerate her small reposed body. They brought with them religious items and even their work tools to touch reverently to her body for blessing, as she was already being considered a saint by many of the faithful. In order to accommodate the continuous stream of visitors of all social classes, burial was delayed and the little nun was reposed for four days. Despite the fact that no artificial means had been used to preserve it, the body remained flexible and the skin retained its rosiness. Perhaps for the first time in her life, Bernadette looked as though she was sleeping peacefully. Her body was then laid quietly in a small chapel of St. Joseph behind the motherhouse, surrounded by grassy hills reminiscent of the ones in Batrès where the young Soubirous once tended her sheep.

4.

LOURDES IN PRINT

The advent of mass communication enabled news of the apparitions of Lourdes to spread quickly throughout the world. In the early days of the events in the grotto, news was reported as it happened in the town's daily newspaper. Readers searched the pages eagerly for the latest on "the Soubirous Affair," a term first coined by Police Commissioner Jacomet. Beyond Lourdes, the story was also finding its way into the pages of numerous other city newspapers.

The story of Bernadette's apparitions received its greatest publicity, however, through a few early and important books, although the works themselves indicated varying perspectives to downright disagreements among the authors. The tale of the Pyrenean peasant, the apparitions, and the miraculous spring with its inexplicable cures was first and most prominently described by journalist and historian Henri Lasserre in 1869. Abbé Peyramale and Bishop Laurence selected Lasserre to chronicle the events at Lourdes for two reasons. First, the man had proven his journalistic abilities through editorial columns that attacked contemporary heresies against the Church. Second, he had experienced a miraculous healing of his eyes that took place at Lourdes in 1863 and hence was a firm believer in the apparitions. Unfortunately, due to the constant demands on his schedule, the project did not take first precedence. In order to hasten the completion of the work, the journalist relied on available legal documents rather than on interviews with actual eyewitnesses.

Lasserre's resulting work, *Notre-Dame de Lourdes*, was published in 1869. It was an attractive book with color illustrations similar in quality to illuminated manuscripts. It was storybook-like in appearance and in content as well, for Lasserre exaggerated the key characters and what he saw as their roles, both good and bad, in the drama. Despite the fact that the book was more of a novel than an exacting historical documentation, Catholics throughout Europe warmly embraced it. In fact, it became the greatest bestseller in the nineteenth century, being translated in more than eighty languages and selling over a million copies by the turn of the century.

Despite the book's popularity and even a papal nod from Pope Pius IX, other writers criticized it for its numerous inaccuracies. Lasserre adamantly opposed any disapproval of his book, claiming that it was the definitive work on the subject of Bernadette and her apparitions. He took particular issue with two of the Garaison Fathers, Pères Sempé and Duboé, who were in the process of writing a new version of the history of Lourdes. It was based on the input of the common folk, although many (including Bernadette's sister Toinette) had gratuitously embellished their accounts. Lasserre, who had not bothered to interview the visionary himself, now visited the ailing nun at Nevers to read to her some portions of the Garaison priests' work. Bernadette protested several of the points, while others were no longer clear in her memory. The journalist, eager to prove his competitors wrong, recorded a list of the visionary's complaints that he submitted to Bishop Laurence and eventually to the Holy Office in Rome. It is interesting to note, however, that he never corrected any of the inaccuracies in his own best-seller.

Next, it was Père Sempé's turn to interview Bernadette. His concern was that she had not read his entire account and could therefore not protest against the overall quality and particular character of the entire work as Lasserre had insinuated. In reviewing the questionable details with the visionary, he realized that much of the information surrounding them had genuinely been forgotten. He saw no reason in making Bernadette sign a statement as the journalist had done. He could see that the young nun was too emotionally fragile at having been brought into the center of such controversy. The details of the story that she could once relate with clarity and confidence now had become clouded, and this filled her with much anguish.

In an effort to quell the public disputes, a third party was brought in, Jesuit Father Leonard Cros, to create a new account that would hopefully capture the truth and the beauty of the apparitions. Cros had been quite moved after meeting Bernadette personally in 1864 and 1865 and was keenly interested in the project. However, his superiors requested that he first finish a history of Jean Berchmans, a Jesuit saint. Therefore, Cros could not begin his work on Lourdes until 1877, but by this time Bernadette had trouble recalling precise details of the apparitions. She would explain to disappointed visitors, "All those things...are already so far back, so long ago. I no longer remember. I do not like to talk about them too much because, my God, what if I made a mistake!"[1]

Cros immersed himself in years of research, interviewing every possible surviving witness of the events, including friends and relatives of Bernadette Soubirous. In total, he questioned more than two hundred people. He also uncovered many diocesan papers and official documents that were thought to have been lost. His efforts to correct and even discredit Lasselle's account ten years prior became almost a preoccupation to the point that he dedicated one of the six volumes he eventually produced specifically to this purpose. What this new author wrote was in some ways so opposing to Lasselle that those who commissioned him were concerned it would cause great confusion among the people and detract from the legitimate spiritual conversion happening at Lourdes. Cros was unwilling to submit to input and revisions on his writing, and as a result only portions of what he wrote were published initially—eight years after his death. It would not be until the centenary of the apparitions that three of his volumes would be published in their original form.

Still another author would arrive on the scene in 1893, except that his contribution, a fictional account entitled simply *Lourdes*, would only further muddy the journalistic waters. Émile Zola was a self-proclaimed atheist and an advocate of secularism. He was of the mindset that the recipients of cures at the grotto were hysterics cured not by the supernatural, but by the power of suggestion. Zola made a fatal mistake in using the stories of real and widely recognized cure recipients and changing their names and outcomes for his book. It cost him greatly. Supposedly, Zola visited these individuals later and offered them a comfortable sum of money before self-exiling himself from France. Although the novel sold well because it was controversial, it did not do much in the long run to offset the fervent devotion that had already taken firm hold in the hearts of Catholics worldwide. Lourdes indeed had made its own chapter in history.

Later, in 1958, in preparation for the centenary of the Sanctuary, Monsignor Pierre-Marie Théas, then bishop of

Tarbes and Lourdes, commissioned Father René Laurentin to write about Lourdes. The world-renowned Marian theologian produced no less than thirty volumes on the subject, and is regarded today as the true and official historian of Bernadette and the apparitions.

PART II
HOPE

5.

THE ADVENT OF PILGRIMAGE

While journalists and clerical hierarchy debated among themselves about what was to be preserved in the pages of history, the faithful continued to come to pray at Lourdes in ever increasing numbers. In the beginning, these pilgrimages were made by individuals or small groups. The first diocesan pilgrimage was organized by Bishop Laurence and consisted of about eight thousand people. It wasn't until 1872, however, that French Catholics would flock to Lourdes in the form of a national pilgrimage. This was inspired by a series of events: the crushing defeat of France by Germany in the Franco-Prussian War, the collapse of Louis Napoleon's Second Empire, and the eruption of antireligious violence—including the murder of an archbishop—ignited by the Paris Commune. On that first major French pilgrimage, Catholics came to Lourdes, some twenty thousand strong, equipped with colorful banners and prepared to pray for the pope, the Church, and their country. Above all, they came to rededicate France to the Virgin Mary for her blessing and protection. Despite vast differences in social backgrounds, religious expression, or political activism, men and women could retreat to the Pyrenees in a united attitude of prayer and penitence. The following year introduced the first foreign pilgrimages from Canada and various parts of Europe.

In those days, pilgrimage was a means to bring Catholics together to pronounce their Christian beliefs peacefully and publicly in opposition to the massive ceremonies organized in the cities by the new French Republic. At first, the possibility of being healed was not a significant motivation behind the pilgrimage movement to Lourdes, but this quickly changed as reports of miraculous cures spread throughout the nation and Europe. The hope for physical cures inspired by Lourdes became such a phenomenon that an Association of Hospitality was established in 1885 specifically to welcome and care for the needs of the sick and debilitated, which by this point had numbered in the thousands. Religious orders and lay organizations worked in tandem to coordinate transportation, hospitalization, and care for sick and dying pilgrims who had somehow managed to endure the heat, the crowds, and the long hours of travel in order to be laid at the feet of the Virgin in the grotto or immersed in the waters of her baths.

The original volunteers of Lourdes were primarily people of noble birth or members of the rich bourgeoisie, as these were the individuals who had the time and financial means to support themselves in their service. In the spirit of true Christianity, the poor and weak were served by the rich and strong, who saw in their less fortunate brothers and sisters the suffering person of Jesus. Physically debilitated individuals— many with infectious diseases—were laid upon mattresses and stretchers across the grotto floor. They were symbols of a hurting humanity, people who had been forsaken by science and medicine that had come to beg God's mercy and healing. Pilgrimage to Lourdes in those early days included little food or sleep, and much intense prayer. Many died at the shrine, some in peace and some in anguish. But the precious few that were able to rise up off their mattresses and walk made the greater impact, hence earning Lourdes the reputation as a pilgrimage place of miracles.

While cures could take place at any moment during a visit to Lourdes, the most common was during the procession of the Blessed Sacrament as it was reverently carried from the basilica to the grotto each evening for Benediction. As the Eucharist encased in a magnificent monstrance was carried past the impassioned crowd, many would rise up, discard their crutches, and join the procession in prayer and thanksgiving. The cliff face of Massabielle was covered with hundreds of these crutches as evidence of the miraculous cures that had taken place there. Historian and author Ruth Harris articulates,

> As the body of Christ was broken to take away sins of the world and to cleanse sinful bodies, so a few pilgrims received the ultimate grace and were cured, in turn becoming whole once again. The procession implicitly linked the Eucharist to the "passions" and "resurrections" among the sick and dying, and for this reason was anticipated with an expectant fervor still palpable on pilgrimage even today.[1]

Another common place for miracles to occur at Lourdes was in the baths or *piscines*. Until the year 1880, there were two provisional pools of spring water for visitors that were filled through the use of a manual pump. To accommodate the growing number of infirm pilgrims seeking to bathe in the spring water in hopes of a healing, a wooden structure was built in 1880 to house fourteen pools. In 1891, the baths were again improved. The walls of the bathing chambers were tiled in blue, a traditional color of the Blessed Mother. Each bath consisted of two compartments, one for the individual to change from street clothes to a towel, and a second containing the actual bath. To access the water, the pilgrim was either lowered on his stretcher or assisted down three steps by two to four assistants. The afflicted person was submerged up to his head in the cold mountain water as prayers were repeated three times to the Holy Virgin.

By immersing themselves in the waters of the spring uncovered by Bernadette, a pilgrim could suddenly experience to his or her astonishment inexplicable improvements in otherwise hopeless medical situations. The majority, however, who braved the frigid waters left much the way they entered, but with a new peaceful acceptance of their suffering. It must never be forgotten that even Bernadette herself, who washed and drank from the same spring, was not spared from years of suffering or a premature death from tuberculosis twenty-one years later. She was known to have recommended Lourdes water for other people's ailments, advising them to take it like medicine with an attitude of genuine faith. However, on her own deathbed at Nevers, she stoically refused offers to receive the same water. The dying visionary understood that a cure and happiness were not a part of the Immaculate Conception's promise for her during her pilgrimage on earth.

Hydrologists concur that the spring unearthed by Bernadette was most likely in existence, as there are many such underground springs feeding the river Gave. According to the reports of Father Leonard Cros, there is some speculation that the spring may have been known to a few of the locals before Bernadette's apparitions. The important point is that the Lady specifically directed Bernadette to dig where the spring lay hidden by mud and river deposits. Furthermore, it wasn't until after it was uncovered in that particular place that miracles began to happen. This is especially mysterious since Lacadé, the town mayor, had the water tested scientifically in the hopes of turning it into a profitable spa, only to discover that it had no special mineral quality whatsoever. Still, astounding miracles continued to take place there.

In addition to Catherine Latapie, whose paralyzed hand was cured, a man named Louis Bouriette washed with the water and received full vision in his right eye, which had been blinded in a quarry explosion. Madame Blaisette Cazenave also received a healing to her eyes after rinsing them in the spring, while a bandage soaked in Lourdes water freed teenager Henri Busquet from painful lesions in his throat. One of the most popular cures involved a Pyrenean peasant who brought her near-death two-year-old son, Justin Bouhort, to the spring. She plunged him into the icy waters—a certain death for such a frail child—and did not even towel him off, hoping to leave the waters on his skin as long as possible. Although bystanders were convinced that the mother had gone mad, her child was fully cured by the next day.

Cures were not limited to those who visited the grotto in person. They also occurred when Lourdes water was brought to the sick or simply when people prayed earnestly for the intercession of Our Lady of Lourdes. One of the most famous "satellite" cases involved a bourgeois adolescent, Mademoiselle Marie Moreau, who had been losing her vision due to an illness. Her family prayed a novena and applied a cloth dipped in Lourdes water to her eyes. Her sight was restored the next day. Later, the family traveled to Lourdes in thanksgiving and to dedicate their daughter to the Virgin. Another authenticated cure involved a Belgian man named Pierre de Rudder. His leg had been crushed by a tree and was infected to the point of requiring amputation. Pierre made a pilgrimage to Oostacker, Belgium, where there was a replica of the Lourdes grotto. His pulverized bones were healed within minutes.

The Episcopal Commission of Inquiry that had been established to investigate the apparitions in 1858 now had the daunting challenge to sift through a barrage of reports of cures to determine which of these were truly medically inexplicable. This was no easy task. Many of the Pyrenean poor could not afford to have a physician, relying on natural remedies instead, and it was impossible to document their preexisting conditions before their cures. Others had not made their ailments known to friends and family, so there was no way to verify changes in their conditions. Initially, the commission consisted entirely of clergy, although it did have access to a medical consultant to help with specific questions, demonstrating a delicate balance between respect for science and trust in the Divine. The first medical consultant was Dr. Vergez, a Catholic physician educated at a notable medical facility in Montpelier and the official inspector for the thermal waters in the Pyrenees. Under his direction, patients were subjected to grueling sessions of questions and physical exams, as the commission carefully recorded their findings.

The Church, represented in the person of Bishop Laurence, had formally authenticated seven miracles at the time of its approval of the apparitions in 1862. Since belief in the prolific number of cures since that time had become so strong among the people, no further moves were made by the ecclesiastic hierarchy to authenticate miracles. Each Sunday from 1867 to 1877, the Garaison Fathers would read aloud narratives of inexplicable healings, much to the astonishment and delight of the audience. As the volume of reported cures escalated, recipients were asked to fill out detailed questionnaires. In time there was a shift toward greater emphasis on medical description and analysis, and by 1878 claims of cures had to be accompanied by a certified diagnosis of the illness.

By 1884, the Lourdes Medical Bureau under the charge of Dr. Dunot de Saint Maclou replaced the Episcopal Commission in the function of investigating and documenting inexplicable cures. It consisted of physicians of international renown, replacing over time the need for a strong clerical presence. The extraordinary number of cure reports prompted Pope Pius X in 1905 to request that the Medical Bureau submit to a proper process the most spectacular cures of Lourdes. The system involved the same firm criteria established in 1734 by Cardinal Lambertini (the future Pope Benedict XIV) to authenticate miracles for the process of canonization. First, the illness had to be determined as grave and severe. Second, no medication was to have been used on the patient (or if it had, it had to be proven ineffective). In addition, the cure had to be instantaneous, nonrecurring, perfect in its completion, and not improved by some earlier determined cause.[2]

In 1908, the fiftieth anniversary of the apparitions at Lourdes, the Church officially added twenty-two miracles to its original list of seven. This action was prompted in part by political pressures to separate Church and state, and to confront a growing attitude of skepticism from the outside world. New French laws demanded the dissolution of communities of religious, forcing the Garaison Fathers to leave the grotto, and the Sanctuary property was transferred to the town in 1910. The bishop and the mayor worked out a compromise to enable the diocese to maintain control of the Domain, but it was a tenuous time. Political forces were not the only ones that threatened the shrine. Hygienists and other medical professionals made several attempts to close Lourdes down on the charges of unsanitary conditions. With so many contagious diseases, they feared it was a perfect breeding ground for infection.

The turn of the century, however, also brought about a turn in thinking. New schools of thought on the self, spirituality, and identity emerged as intellectual trends attempted to understand the significance of religious, spiritual, and occult experience. Lourdes became an object of study among secular psychiatrists, psychologists, physicians, and scientists. The shrine was given a further boost when the Church simultaneously initiated the process for Bernadette's beatification and canonization that would eventually give Sister Marie-Bernard a new name: St. Bernadette.

6.

FROM SEER TO SAINT

The process of distinguishing saints in the Catholic Church is a meticulous one that involves several stages with strict criteria. Once a candidate's name is submitted to and approved by the local authority (usually the bishop), the cause is considered opened and the candidate is given the title *Servant of God*. The initial goal is to gather the testimonies of numerous witnesses to resolve whether the person in question has indeed led a virtuous life. If enough evidence is gathered, the title *Venerable* is conferred upon the candidate. In order to proceed to the next stage—beatification—it must be verified that a miracle (typically a physical healing) has occurred as a result of someone praying specifically for that candidate's intercession. If this is found to be true, the candidate is beatified and earns the designation *Blessed*. This means that the person may be venerated by his local church. Canonization, the final stage in which the Church declares the candidate *Saint*, requires two attested miracles and permits veneration by the universal Church. Canonization is an infallible statement by the Church that the saint is in heaven.

The official opening of the process for beatification of Bernadette Soubirous was delayed until after the death of Mother Vauzou at her own request. In her opinion, Bernadette did not fit the mold of saint either in intellect, personality, or important accomplishments. Therefore, it wasn't until 1907, twenty-eight years after Bernadette's death, that the initial phase of the process began. For two years, information was gathered from witnesses on the life, virtues, reputation for saintliness, and miracles of the young French nun and visionary.

From an outward appearance, Bernadette did not seem to be greatly introspective. Nor was she known to be particularly eloquent in her speech or in her letters. In fact, over time, the seer became quite reserved about her comments and her feelings, and for this reason she is often referred to as the most secretive of all the saints. In studying the private notes of Bernadette, however, one discovers a surprising maturity and depth to her spirituality. For example, she often wrote in her notebooks about a desire to suffer with Jesus. She continually looked for sacrifices to offer for sinners and the souls in purgatory, one of these being her constant trips to the parlor to receive visitors. She expressed a private aspiration to live a hidden life like Jesus and the Blessed Mother. Finally, she recognized the responsibility that came with the tremendous graces she had received, and in her heart she longed to be a great saint. She wrote,

> My divine spouse has made me desire a humble and hidden life. Jesus has often told me that I will not die until I have sacrificed all to him. And to convince me, he has often told me that when it is over, at the hour of death, he alone, Jesus crucified, will console me. I will carry only him, my faithful friend, with me to my grave. It is madness to attach myself to anything other than him.[1]

It can be said that Bernadette did not accomplish any significant feats or leave behind any literary masterpieces. Rather, it was her hidden life of holiness, obedience, patience, and simplicity—and her holy death—that testified to her worthiness for the investigation. As Abbé Febvre, Bernadette's last confessor, would note:

> When the humble Bernadette knocked at the door of the convent of the Sisters of Nevers...she already possessed certain lights, certain teachings, and a line of conduct that would give her direction and also help her spiritual directors and superiors to guide her on the pathways to perfection. Meditating on the words, recommendations, and secrets communicated to her by the Immaculate Conception and acquiring a deeper understanding of the mysterious actions she performed in the grotto, Bernadette would formulate rules of conduct that would enable her to arrive at the ideal of sanctity asked of her.
>
> Moreover, like the prophets of the old law whose lives and actions were a visible confirmation of the great truths they proclaimed, Bernadette's mission would not just be to transmit the wishes of heaven. She would also practice works that gave expression to this message. Her habitual state of suffering would reveal to souls the pathway and the necessity of suffering for those who wished to be "happy not in this world but in the other."[2]

Abbé Pomian, her first confessor, made a striking comment when he said, "The best proof of the apparitions is Bernadette herself."[3] Bishop Laurence would elaborate on this in his pastoral letter acknowledging the authenticity of the apparitions in 1862:

Who on drawing near her cannot but admire the simplicity, the nobility, and the modesty of this child? While everyone was talking about the marvels that had been revealed, she alone remained silent. She spoke only when questioned; then she related all, with no affectation, with a touching innocence; and to the many questions asked of her, without hesitation she gave clear, precise answers, to the point and marked by a strong conviction. Subjected to severe tests, she was never shaken by threats. To the most generous offers, she replied with a noble indifference. Ever true to herself, in the various interrogations she was put through, she constantly adhered to what she had already said, without ever adding or retracting anything. Bernadette's sincerity is therefore unquestionable....It is unquestioned. Her opponents, when she had any, have themselves given her this compliment.[4]

According to protocol, on September 22, 1909, in the presence of ecclesiastical and civil authorities, two physicians, and the entire congregation of the Sisters of Nevers, Bernadette's remains were exhumed from the chapel of St. Joseph for identification. Despite the fact that it had been thirty years since the visionary was buried and no embalming had taken place according to the rule of the order, her face and body were remarkably preserved. The doctors in attendance issued the following report:

The coffin was open in the presence of the Bishop of Nevers, the mayor of the town, his principal deputy, several canons, and ourselves. We noticed no smell. The body was clothed in the habit of

Bernadette's order. The habit was damp. Only the face, hands, and forearms were uncovered. The head was tilted to the left. The face was matt white. The skin clung to the muscles and the muscles adhered to the bones. The sockets of the eyes were covered by the eyelids. The brows were flat on the skin and stuck to the arches above the eyes. The lashes of the right eyelid were stuck to the skin. The nose was dilated and shrunken. The mouth was open slightly, and it could be seen that the teeth were still in place. The hands, which were crossed on her breast, were perfectly preserved, as were the nails. The hands still held a rusting Rosary. The veins on the forearms stood out.

Like the hands, the feet were wizened and the toenails were still intact (one of them was torn off when the corpse was washed). When the habits had been removed and the veil lifted from the head, the whole of the shriveled body could be seen, rigid and taut in every limb. It was found that the hair, which had been cut short, was stuck to the head and still attached to the skull—that the ears were in a state of perfect preservation—that the left-hand side of the body was slightly higher than the right from the hip up. The stomach had caved in and was taut like the rest of the body. It sounded like cardboard when struck. So rigid was the body that it could be rolled over and back for washing. The lower parts of the body had turned slightly black. This seems to have been the result of the carbon of which quite large quantities were found in the coffin.

In witness of which we have duly drawn up
this present statement in which all is truthfully
recorded.

Nevers, 22 September, 1909,
Dr. Ch. David, A. Jourdan[5]

While the Church looks upon incorruption as a special
favor from God, it does not implicitly indicate a miracle.
Therefore, after the examination, the sisters removed the
body, washed it quickly, and redressed it in a new habit. It
was then laid in a new coffin lined with zinc and returned
to the same tomb below the pavement of St. Joseph's where
it would remain for ten more years. In 1913, Pope Pius X
signed the decree for the introduction of the Cause of the
Servant of God, and conferred upon Bernadette the title of
Venerable. Due to a delay caused by World War I, the apostolic process did not begin until 1917. Two years later, the
body was exhumed for a second time. It was found to be in
much the same state of preservation as before.

In 1923, Pope Pius XI announced the heroic virtues of
Bernadette, publicly declaring, "There is no doubt that here
we are in the presence of saintliness in the exact and precise
sense of the word. Indeed, when we consider the life of
Bernadette as it has emerged from all phases of the
Process…it can be summed up in three words: Bernadette
was faithful to her mission, she was humble in her glory,
and she was strong when she was put to the test."[6] When
the body was exhumed for a third and final time in 1925, it
had begun to undergo the normal process of decay. There
was some slight discoloration to the face and parts of the body
caused by a residue of soap left behind from the hasty washing by the nuns ten years prior, as well as the repeated expo-

sures of the body to the air. The attending surgeon, Dr. Comte, made the following observations:

> From this examination I conclude that the body of the Venerable Bernadette is intact, the skeleton is complete, the muscles have atrophied, but are well preserved; only the skin, which has shriveled, seems to have suffered from the effects of the damp in the coffin. It has taken on a grayish tinge and is covered with patches of mildew and quite a large number of crystals and calcium salts; but the body does not seem to have putrefied, nor has any decomposition of the cadaver set in, although this would be expected and normal after such a long period in a vault hollowed out of the earth.[7]

After a few precious relics were removed—two ribs, part of the liver and diaphragm, and two kneecaps—the body was wrapped in bandages, leaving only the face and hands exposed. It was not embalmed. Due to the darkening of some spots on the skin, however, a decision was made to cover the face and hands with a light coating of wax for a more aesthetic appearance. From that point on, Bernadette's body was reposed in a casket of glass and gold in the chapel of Saint-Gildard at Nevers, where it remains to this day for the faithful to venerate. That same year, in a grand and solemn ceremony at St. Peter's Basilica in Rome, Pope Pius XI beatified her in the presence of hundreds of thousands of Catholics, including her youngest brother, Pierre Soubirous. Eight years later, this same pope canonized Bernadette. The date was December 8, 1933, the feast of the Immaculate Conception.

While the humble nun may be one of the most beautifully preserved saints known, what is more important than

the inexplicable escape from decay at death is the living testimony of this saint. It is worthwhile to note, for example,
that after Bernadette's apparitions in Lourdes, nearly two
hundred reports were filed claiming visions of the Virgin
Mary. None of these claims, however, could be substantiated. In each case, Bernadette was held as the model in
which to measure the others because of her exemplary
behavior. This is a fact that still holds true today. It can be
said that until the end, she never added a single detail to her
testimony, she did not seek self-recognition, she submitted
willingly to authority, and she patiently suffered the disbelief and accusations of others. In sum, Bernadette earned
her sainthood, not because she saw visions, but because of
her heroic virtue in responding to God's mysterious call.[8]

Bernadette Soubirous,
Pyrenean peasant.
Photographer unknown.

The grotto of Massabielle in 1858.
Photo by M. Viron.

The grotto at night.
Photo by Mark Ficocelli.

Water taps provide
Lourdes water for
drinking and washing.
Photo by author.

The statue in the niche where Bernadette first saw the Lady. *Photo by Paul McMahon.*

Votive candles burn continually in the grotto area. *Photo by author.*

A tiled plaque marks the place Bernadette knelt during
the first apparition.
Photo by Mark Ficocelli.

Hospitality volunteer Teresa Eversoll demonstrates proper lifting
and transferring techniques.
Photo by author.

A plaque commemorates John Paul II's two visits to
Lourdes.
Photo by Michael Kerrigan, CSP.

Pilgrims often leave flowers and prayer petitions at the source of
the spring.
Photo by Mark Ficocelli.

The Rosary Basilica and Rosary Square.
Photo by Paul McMahon.

The crown on the dome
of the Rosary Basilica.
*Photo by
Mark Ficocelli.*

The Basilica of the Immaculate Conception with its expansive ramping systems.
Photo by Mark Ficocelli.

The crowned statue of Mary in the Esplanade.
Photo by Paul McMahon.

The Blessed Sacrament Procession occurs daily between the months of April and October.
Photo by M. Lacaze.

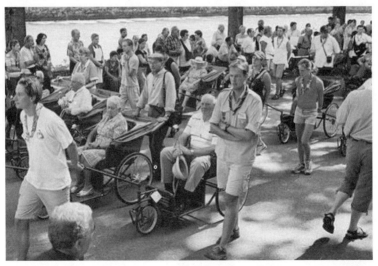

Thousands of volunteers assist pilgrims with illness and disability.
Photo by M. Durand.

The Torchlight Procession begins at the grotto, travels down the Esplanade, and convenes at Rosary Square.
Photographer unknown.

Taking part in the Torchlight Procession.
Photo by Mark Ficocelli.

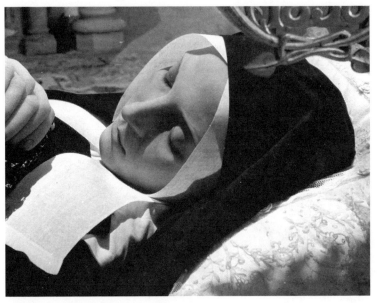

The incorrupt body of St. Bernadette.
Photographer unknown.

For most people, the young shepherdess is how they will always remember Bernadette Soubirous.
Photo by Michael Kerrigan, CSP.

7.

AUTHENTICATED MIRACLES

Since the days of Bernadette's apparitions, Lourdes has rightfully earned a reputation as a place where the miraculous happens. The mere mention of the name still conjures up images today of the lame walking and the blind seeing. But the sudden return of health to a gravely ill individual that can—and does—happen at the shrine is only a small part of the overall mystery. People, after all, are drawn to Lourdes for a multitude of reasons. Certainly many pilgrims come for physical healing and relief. Many, however, come with tortured minds and spirits. Some seek to find the grace to change their lives and free themselves from the bondage of materialism, addiction, and other self-enslavement. Others are burdened with mental illness. Still others come for an increase of faith or because they have lost their faith altogether. For those who come to Lourdes in emotional anguish and return home with peace-filled hearts, it can certainly seem miraculous. To be deemed an *authentic* miracle, however, according to the tradition of the Church, it is a different matter altogether.

The Catholic Church still utilizes the same criteria established by Cardinal Lambertini in 1734 for the process of authenticating miracles. In the nineteenth century, this model was quite workable. In the twenty-first century, however, with the advancements in medical science and its practice, the formula has become more troublesome. In addition, the process of authenticating miracles is costly and time consuming, and many bishops feel that enough miracles have already been approved. This in part helps to explain why, out of seven thousand cases of inexplicable cures on file with the Lourdes Medical Bureau today, the Church has only recognized sixty-seven of them as miraculous.

According to Dr. Patrick Theillier, the current medical director of the Lourdes Medical Bureau, the small number of Church-approved cures is the result of three factors. First, the 1734 criteria exclude spiritual and psychological cures, as these cannot be measured scientifically. Needless to say, there are innumerable healings and conversions of this nature resulting from prayers or pilgrimages to Lourdes that have never been documented at all. Second, not everyone who receives a profound improvement in his or her physical health wishes to undergo the intense and lengthy examination process required for a cure to be authenticated. Consequently, many pilgrims who are convinced they have been cured through the intercession of Our Lady of Lourdes return home quietly without ever presenting themselves to be archived. Third, a significant amount of the scientifically inexplicable cures that have been reported and are on file with the Medical Bureau lack some requirement to allow them to advance to the final stage. Among these, in the doctor's professional opinion, there are at least 2,500 cases that are considered truly remarkable.

Dr. Theillier says you only need to look at the extraordinary number of plaques that line the walls of the Upper Basilica and crypt expressing gratitude for favors received to begin to appreciate how prayers have been answered at Lourdes. But the phenomenon is not by any means limited to the past. The fact is, the Medical Bureau receives more reports today than ever before from people all over the world claiming that they have received the grace of a physical cure. Dr. Theillier says:

> The physical cures declared to the Medical Bureau are only the visible ones, ones you can analyze objectively. However, they serve to reveal, recall or confirm all the other kinds of cures, the invisible ones, healing of the mind and spirit, which many people claim to undergo on pilgrimage to Lourdes. True, many sick persons go home in the same physical condition—but radiant with a joy that totally transfigures their state of mind and leaves us astounded. What we are witnessing there is a transformation of their inner experiences, leaving them stronger to live through their sufferings, their illnesses, their handicaps. This completely defies medical analysis.[1]

> Because of Divine intervention and Mary's meditation in this holy place [he writes elsewhere], Lourdes is a powerful and permanent center of healing. Here we have a Christian community assembled; people of all nations, ethnic groups, races, languages, the well and the sick (recognized as persons in their own right); this community is united in faith, prayer, charity, and alms, in a place where once Bernadette saw heaven open….Here, we can lay down our burdens, reveal our wounds, make our gestures of faith, free of charge, and in a concrete, meaningful way. Everyone is free to go where he or she likes—the grotto, the pools, the Way of the

Cross, to Adoration of the Blessed Sacrament, and especially to the Chapel of Reconciliation. Here, today, heaven still opens for everyone![2]

The medical director explains that people whose cures have been recognized as miraculous serve as powerful witnesses to the faith. It is, after all, an extraordinary event to realize that one has been touched by God. Life is never the same after. However, faith is not a prerequisite for healing—at least not individual faith. It is the faith of the people that God gathers in this unique and sacred place, together with their faith, prayers, and acts of compassion, that form the Body of Christ, which in itself is capable of healing. In Lourdes, healing can happen to anyone. Atheists and people of other faiths have reported cures. The doctor cited a recent example of a Muslim man suffering with Crohn's Disease for twelve years. He had ten surgical interventions and problems with abscesses and other complications. At the time he came to Lourdes, he was on sixteen milligrams of cortisone for the pain. After going through the baths in 2004, the man was able to stop taking the medication immediately, an impossibility for someone on that amount of cortisone. The case is currently being investigated, and the individual is in the process of requesting Baptism.

Dr. Theillier feels frustrated at times over the exorbitant time it can take to investigate and recognize cures. In one case it took fifty-five years for a cure to be officially deemed miraculous. "It is not satisfactory at all to have to wait for decades for a healing to be recognized," he told me. "This is the time when the Church needs to be a spiritual witness for the current times we are living in. Today's world needs these kinds of witnesses."

In an effort to present a more balanced picture of the impressive outcomes that continue to take place at Lourdes, the Medical Bureau, in conjunction with the bishop, has been working to revolutionize cure reporting and evaluation. To appreciate this more fully, it is helpful to understand the traditional procedure of reporting a cure at Lourdes.

Traditionally, the process would begin when a person approached the Medical Bureau upon receipt of a rapid and inexplicable improvement in his or her condition. At that point, the person would be required to recount the details to the team of physicians who happened to be serving the bureau at the time. (It is a policy that any medical professional, no matter his or her faith—or lack thereof—is welcome to serve on the Medical Bureau while visiting Lourdes. An estimated five hundred physicians assist in this capacity each year.)

If an individual's story sounded credible, a dossier would be opened and the "cured" person would be invited to return in a year's time with complete medical records and a doctor's report. The cure recipient would then be examined and questioned a second time by the present team of doctors making up the Medical Bureau. If necessary, the candidate could be asked to return a third time with any additional records that might be required. The lapse in time—generally five years—would help to ensure that the cure was complete and lasting, important criteria for authenticating a miracle. Next, the medical director would then select the most promising cases to submit to the International Medical Committee of Lourdes, a panel established in 1947 that consists of twenty Catholic physicians from highly respected medical facilities around the world. This committee meets annually in Paris, with the bishop of Tarbes and Lourdes serving as a cochair with a medical specialist of his choosing. The meetings typically begin with a Mass, followed by a presentation of the dossiers by the medical director. A member or two of the International Medical Committee would be assigned to each case and it would become their responsibility to meet with the patient and his or her physician. Typically, the investigation could take years to ensure that all records were accurate. At the end, the committee would vote on the cases to be presented to the Church.

To reach this point in the process, the patient's medical condition would have had to be considered medically inexplicable by numerous doctors around the world. Still, it would not yet be considered a miracle. For that, the Church must be involved. The final step would be for the case to go to the patient's local bishop. This is where many cases have run into difficulty. It is not uncommon for a bishop to completely ignore the inquiry because of his personal avoidance of the subject of supernatural miracles. It is also not uncommon for a bishop to appoint his own medical advisor to review the documentation, which may require the case to go back to square one despite all previous medical approval.

On October 22–24, 1993, an International Congress was held at Lourdes to discuss the topic of cures and to specifically address the criteria that have long been used to recognize a miraculous event. It was quickly acknowledged that modern medicine posed numerous complexities in the traditional process of determining a miracle. For example, few physicians today would willingly declare a particular disease or condition as incurable, one of Lambertini's mandatory criteria. Modern physicians are more comfortable speaking in statistical terms, giving patients and their families an approximate percentage on the odds of improvement or survival. Also unrealistic today is the likelihood of a patient receiving no previous medical treatment before his or her cure. Quite the contrary; it is hoped that every person suffering from illness and disability today has been afforded the best medical science has to offer. Still another obstacle is the idea of "instantaneous" cures, which rules out rapid progressive improvement.

At the end of their meeting, the International Congress concluded that a healing is miraculous when two conditions exist: one, that its explanation is beyond the usual rules of medicine or the normal course of the disease; and two, that it brings the patient and witnesses to believe that the healing was due to God's special intervention. This second part of the declaration—the profound spiritual effect on the individual—has long been underrated in the evaluation process. Now it was something to be seriously considered.

The gross imbalance between the number of cures reported (and not reported) versus the conservative number of miracles authenticated by the Church has resulted in a landmark decision by the International Medical Committee. After their November 2005 annual meeting, the committee, under the leadership of Bishop Jacques Perrier and his cochair, Professor Francois-Bernard Michel, voted to modify their evaluation procedures. The new process now consists of three stages. It begins in much the same way as before, when a person who believes he or she was healed through the Virgin's intercession makes a voluntary and spontaneous statement to the Medical Bureau. A council then evaluates the claim to examine the progression of the disease and the patient's character in order to determine if the cure is clearly beyond the normal medical provisions of the illness in question. The council summarizes their findings for each case by categorizing it as "not for follow-up," "pending," or "unexpected cure."

Once a cure is categorized as "unexpected," the bishop from the claimant's diocese is informed and the case advances to the second stage. Here, numerous experts and specialists pour over relevant scientific literature, comparing it to the existing medical documents to determine whether the cure is truly unusual. In the third and final stage, the Lambertini criteria helps to ensure that the cure of a serious condition with an unfavorable prognosis has been found complete and lasting and has taken place in a sudden and unexpected manner. If the International Medical Committee concludes that based on the current state of scientific knowledge the cure is recognized as exceptional, the case is submitted to the bishop of Tarbes and Lourdes and to the healed person's bishop for final approval. Dr. Theillier is optimistic about this new procedure for recognition of cures in Lourdes:

> The new procedure allows the cured person to be accompanied so that he or she is no longer alone in carrying this experience of healing, which is not always easy to live through both in terms of the media and the entourage. It also enables the person to offer a valid testimony to the community of the faithful and it gives the cured person the opportunity for a first act of thanksgiving. Most importantly, we hope that the new procedures will ultimately lead to the realization that cures that are visible, bodily, and physical are signs of the innumerable interior and spiritual cures, not visible, which everyone can experience here.[3]

For the first time, the International Medical Committee plans to reflect on the pertinence of healing in cases involving psychological and mental diseases, as many people have been greatly unburdened and given fresh perspectives after a pilgrimage to Lourdes. Equally significant, Bishop Perrier made newspaper headlines in March 2006 by announcing at a press conference that he is drafting a new proposal regarding healings that he plans to submit to the Vatican for approval. According to the bishop, the proposal does not request changing current Church policies and traditions on authenticating *miracles*. Rather, it seeks to establish a new category—"authenticated *healings*"—that will enable recipients to share their stories of physical improvement and spiritual conversion in their parishes and on retreats, something they do not have Church approval to do currently. The new category will by no means reduce the stringent evaluation process. The person's condition will still need to be medically verified as serious and its reversal as scientifically inexplicable. It will, however, feature for the first time the added dimension of assessing the spiritual benefits that are bestowed by the healing. Bishop Perrier explained his actions:

> If we take the person into consideration, what is important is the fact that he regained his health and that the event occurred in the context of prayer, his or that of his entourage, as in the Gospels. I wish that, in this type of situation, the person might be allowed to testify to the grace received. To recognize the authenticity of the Apparitions of 1858, Bishop Laurence…was never able to verify in a scientific and indisputable way that something had happened in the grotto of Massabielle, but after a four year investigation on the personality, the acts and deeds of Bernadette, the Bishop concluded that her testimony was trustworthy. It is my wish that the bishops who have a person in their diocese who was unquestionably cured in Lourdes, should

authenticate their testimony after the other criteria are properly fulfilled.[4]

Vittorio Micheli from Scurelle, Italy, is one of the living recipients of a cure that has been recognized as miraculous by the Catholic Church. Informally, he is referred to as "Miracle Number 63." In 1962 when he was twenty-two and serving in the military, Mr. Micheli was discovered to have a malignant tumor on the left side of his pelvis. The cancer had eaten away much of his left hip and left him in excruciating pain. The disease was spreading rapidly through his body, and the doctors declared him to be terminal. To please his brother, Mr. Micheli agreed to go to Lourdes, but in truth he was rather indifferent about the whole matter. During his pilgrimage, nothing notable happened, except that he bathed his good leg, as his affected leg was in a cast from the pelvis to the foot.

When he returned home, Mr. Micheli experienced a rapid return to health. His appetite came back and his chronic pain subsided. Within two months he was able to walk again, and X rays revealed a remarkable and inexplicable *reconstruction* of his hip. Since 1963, the Italian cure recipient has returned to Lourdes every year. He is a familiar face at the Sanctuary, serving as a stretcher bearer, or *brancardier*, to serve other afflicted pilgrims who come to Lourdes in search of healing. In 1976, after years of study by the Medical Bureau and the International Medical Committee, Vittorio Micheli's case was submitted to the Church and received the recognition of being miraculous.

Today Mr. Micheli is an unassuming man who does not talk much about his miracle in public. He was gracious enough to share a few words by telephone, via a translator, about how his cure has affected him today. "I am no different than anyone else," he said. "I didn't do anything to deserve this miracle. I didn't have it for me—I had it for others, so that they might believe. I only went to Lourdes that first time to please my brother. My doctors had advised against it. I did not go there to ask for the grace to be healed. That was the Lord's plan. The experience has improved my Christian life, of course. I try to do good. I am sensitive to people who suffer, and I go on pilgrimage to Lourdes very frequently in thanksgiving for my cure. When people ask my advice, I do not feel qualified to give any. I simply tell them to ask for strength in their suffering."

Dr. Theillier adds these further words on miracles:

Most people think of miracles as the impossible actually taking place. More importantly, miracles are events associated with God, who is all around us and who wishes good upon us. He loves us very much and sometimes chooses to use these external signs to confirm that in us….We often don't notice these signs because in our materially developed society, we tend to believe that what matters is what we ourselves have or can do: Are we strong? Do we have money in the bank? Do we have adequate material means? Because of this, we have lost the sense of the sacred—something that remains to a large degree, for example, in Africa. When I meet with Africans at various conferences, they tell me that there are many miracles in their native lands. "We don't even mention them much," they say, "because so many of them occur. We don't have the medicines that are available in the West, so we pray over the sick and they get healed."[5]

For Dr. Theillier, the subject of miracles will always pose intrigue. A miracle, after all, is not something that can be precisely squared off in a little box. If we seek to prove a miracle, he explains, it is no longer a miracle. He acknowledges that there will always be skeptics, but reminds us that even the faithful are not obligated to accept the miracles or the apparitions. It is not part of our doctrine of faith—the Church merely invites us to believe. He quotes Christian apologist Blaise Pascal who summed it up best when he said, "There is enough light for those who desire only to see, and enough darkness for those with a contrary disposition."

8.

SPIRITUAL CONVERSION

While much publicity has been given to the physical cures and miracles that have taken place at Lourdes, far less has been printed about the spiritual conversions that occur at the Sanctuary on a daily basis. Since spiritual conversion is an essential part of the message of Bernadette and her apparitions, I would be remiss not to devote a chapter to this special dynamic.

The spiritual dimension of a pilgrimage to Lourdes—the most important aspect—is facilitated by the presence of a priest, either one that accompanies the organized pilgrimages or one that is stationed at the shrine as part of a permanent body of chaplains. The Community of Chaplains at Lourdes, some thirty members strong, is made up of diocesan priests together with religious priests and brothers from various congregations and societies. They serve on a rotational basis at the personal invitation of the bishop of Tarbes and Lourdes. The responsibility of the chaplains is to welcome and serve pilgrims from all over the world. A unique characteristic of the community is its international flavor. In order to welcome pilgrims from different nations, the priests must be able to speak either Italian, Spanish, English, German, or Dutch (or a combination of the above), as these, together with French, are the six official languages of the Sanctuary.

Chaplains at Lourdes serve as the pastoral ministers of the shrine. It is their responsibility to facilitate pilgrimage through participation in the sacraments and the ceremonies. Specifically, the chaplains celebrate the Mass and the Sacrament of Reconciliation, they lead pilgrims in prayers such as the Rosary and Stations of the Cross, and they help to organize the processionals. They may also be given assignments in specific ministries such as Daily Pilgrimage Service, Hospitality, Youth Service, or they may serve on commissions responsible for matters such as liturgy and sacred art. In addition to these responsibilities, it is imperative that the chaplains understand and can communicate the message of Lourdes as it was received from Bernadette. During the pilgrimage season from April to October, approximately 120 priests come to Lourdes as auxiliary confessors to support the busy chaplains in their work.

Father Raymond Zambelli is the rector at Lourdes. As such, he is the bishop's closest assistant and full-time representative at the Sanctuary and is responsible for some four hundred paid employees as well as the community of thirty chaplains living at the shrine. His mission is to preserve the message of the Blessed Virgin in all its purity, to pass it on faithfully, and to give the opportunity for pilgrims around the world to be welcomed and moved by piety and faith. Father Zambelli came to Lourdes in 2003 after serving as the rector for the Sanctuary of Lisieux for ten years. The experience, he told me, helped prepare him for his current position. He said, "The Sanctuary at Lisieux is less important than Lourdes in that it only welcomes about a million pilgrims each year from around the world compared to the six million that come here. But both are places of inspiration, faith, and miracles. Lisieux has enabled me to experience the universal Church, which is an important aspect of Lourdes. Working with different people in different capacities has allowed me to hone my pastoral, managing, and material organizational skills in order to guide a diversity of pilgrims in a spiritual way and manage a sanctuary."

Father Zambelli has a deep respect and admiration for both French saints Thérèse and Bernadette. "I remain touched by the spirituality of Thérèse of Lisieux, which is based on trust and love. Her simplicity and depth has affected me both as a Christian and as a priest. The Little Flower has helped me to understand that to love is the secret of the human experience and the key to happiness. Bernadette has also touched me because of her humility and her authentic love for Our Lady and for sinners. In many ways, Bernadette and Thérèse are very much alike, and because of that, she is now also a sister for me."

The rector notes that physical healings and cures attributed to Lourdes are only the tip of the iceberg of the genuine spiritual conversion that affects pilgrims in a deep and lasting way. "At Lourdes," he says, "the Virgin Mary asks us to live in consistency with our consciences, with our baptism, with our faith, and with the Good News. The true spiritual stakes of a pilgrimage are to welcome this call to consistency. Many people answer affirmatively and allow the Virgin Mary to help them unite their souls to hers."

Experiencing conversion is one thing; keeping it alive after the pilgrimage is another matter. "To protect and nurture the grace of conversion received in Lourdes," says Father Zambelli, "we need to pray day after day with humility. Nothing lasts forever. The spiritual life is a constant battle. The evil one never gives up trying to keep us from choosing the right way. We need the assistance of the Blessed Virgin who defeats him and the protection of the sacraments of the Church."

Father Marcel-Emard Duguay currently serves as one of the Sanctuary's permanent chaplains. He is a Eudist father of the Congregation of Jesus and Mary, an ecclesiastical society founded in 1643 in France by Saint John Eudes. Father Duguay hails from New Brunswick, Canada. He came to Lourdes in 2002 when his community was invited by the bishop to serve at the shrine. Since their religious house was rather small, it was decided to send an international community of Eudist Fathers to Lourdes, with Father Duguay serving as the North American representative. He was joined by three Eudist priests—one from Colombia, one from Africa, and one from France—and given a commission to serve at the shrine for three years. At the end of their term, the bishop invited Father Duguay to remain longer at Lourdes if he so desired because of his ability to speak French, Italian, and English. With permission from his community, he accepted the offer.

Today, Father Duguay serves as a chaplain to the Hospitality of Our Lady of Lourdes (a service that will be discussed in the next chapter). In this function, he works with volunteers from around the world in welcoming pilgrims with illness and disability to the Sanctuary. The chaplain's role, however, is not focused on training hospitality members in techniques such as how to handle the sick at the train station or at the baths, or how to prepare beds and wash dishes. His role, rather, is to assist with the spiritual aspect of the volunteers' commitment. Specifically, he introduces the volunteers-in-training to the message of Lourdes, he talks about the concept of spiritual welcoming and spiritual accompaniment, he speaks about commitment and suffering, and he addresses the "after-pilgrimage" experience.

As priest and chaplain, Father Duguay shared with me some of his own personal observations regarding the unique spiritual aspect of Lourdes. "In order to understand Lourdes," he explains, "you have to look at who Bernadette was and what was said to her in the grotto. In truth, not many words were actually said here. The Lady, after all, did not speak much. On top of that, there was nothing new said here. The key to deciphering the true message of Lourdes, therefore, lies with Bernadette herself."

The chaplain acknowledged that many people are aware of the physical poverty suffered by Bernadette and her family. They were desperately poor. But Bernadette also suffered a spiritual poverty, a poverty that was much more significant. She had two basic hungers beyond the natural and expected hunger for physical food. Her first hunger was to learn the word of God, but she was denied this treasure by her inability to speak French or to read or write. She knew, certainly, how to pray. But to answer a question about God and to understand who He was required her to learn her catechism, and this was a great obstacle for the young girl. Bernadette's second burning hunger was her desire to eat the bread of life through the reception of Holy Communion. But this, too, was beyond her grasp due to her academic insufficiency.

"If you recall," says Father Duguay, "right before the apparitions, Bernadette had been living in Batrès. She was sent there because of the family's desperate situation, but also on the condition that she would be able to learn her catechism. This would not materialize, of course, for the parish priest left to join a monastery and Madame Laguës was not patient enough to teach her poor student. Bernadette knew that Lourdes held the answer to seek what she desired spiritually. Her desire for the Eucharist motivated her to leave the comforts of Batrès for the poverty of home. When she was finally able to return to Lourdes, she found herself once again facing cold and hunger. It was this cold and hunger that lured her to Massabielle to find wood that day in February. She had never been there before. It was, in a way, a mysterious call to the grotto."

The chaplain pointed to the similarity between Bernadette and today's pilgrim. "In order to be a pilgrim at Lourdes," he continued, "and enter into the Sanctuary as a Christian, you need to have a void inside, like Bernadette had. This void, this poverty, allows a place for Jesus. Bernadette always said after the apparitions that Our Lady chose her because she was the poorest and most ignorant of all. I think she was also chosen for her openness and for her deep longing for Jesus. What happened to Bernadette at the grotto is what happens to all pilgrims who are earnestly seeking—Our Lady ultimately leads them to her son, particularly through the sacraments."

To illustrate, Father Duguay demonstrated the fact that immediately after the initial encounter with the Lady, Bernadette went to the priest to speak about her experience at the grotto, and then made her first Confession. In this important sacrament, she experienced Jesus, as all Catholics do when they receive the Sacrament of Reconciliation. She also continued to go to school to prepare for her First Communion. On June 3, 1858, just before the last apparition, her wish at last became a reality. She received First Communion. Through Our Lady, therefore, Bernadette was led to the Son and her hunger was satisfied.

The Lady's request for a procession and a chapel was highly significant, according to Father Duguay. "The chapel was understood as a building to be built. But we must remember that the Church is above all the people of God. This Church is always in the making. Here, at Lourdes, people come from all over the world, in procession, in pilgrimage. Here, every day, the Church—God's people—at the invitation of Mary, is built around the Eucharist and the sacrament of forgiveness. Then, the pilgrims return to their native lands where the Church continues to be in the making."

In examining Bernadette's actions at the grotto since her first encounter with the Lady, the Canadian chaplain pointed out, it becomes clear that Lourdes is first and foremost a place of prayer. Each time Bernadette returned to Massabielle, she would kneel, make the Sign of the Cross, and pray the Rosary. The prayer was specific and deliberate. The most important message the visionary received in her apparitions was to do penance and to pray for sinners. The Lady said, "Penance, Penance, Penance! Pray for the conversion of sinners....Kiss the ground for the conversion of sinners....Go to the fountain, drink and wash in it....Eat the grass that grows there." Therefore, Lourdes also becomes a place of conversion. This appeal for conversion is the core of the message of Lourdes—not just individual conversion, but conversion within the Church. In order to do penance, one must truly change one's heart and convert from previous ways. Today, a century and a half later, the Virgin Mary continues to invite all people to pray and do penance. In response, multitudes of people have returned from Lourdes with "new hearts."

Father Duguay noted emphatically that the peace and serenity of mind and soul that people discover at Lourdes is as important as the astonishing physical manifestations. "You won't find these spiritual miracles framed on the walls of the Medical Bureau," he admitted, "but they are imprinted forever on the hearts of the recipients. The Chapel of Reconciliation, for example, is a place for miracles. I know that, because I serve there. I cannot give you details, but I've seen more people than I can count come into that place frightened and stressed, but when they leave, the tears that flow are tears of joy. I've seen people who have been away from the Church for forty or fifty years embrace the faith with everything they have. These are true miracles."

Another chaplain, Father Liam Griffin, an Irish-born priest of the Oblates of Mary Immaculate, attests to the astonishing healings that occur within the confines of the Chapel of Reconciliation (or the "Miracle Bureau," as our pilgrimage director aptly dubbed it). When I caught up with him at Lourdes, he was just finishing a ten-year service at the Sanctuary, where he has been responsible for seeing that the English language is used properly in the international celebrations and in the sacraments. Father Griffin told me, "I often get the question, have I seen any miracles? And I answer, yes, or course. Hundreds. We see people having life-changing experiences at Lourdes all the time, especially in the Reconciliation Chapel. Our Lady's call here is to change and come back to the Gospel. It is the interior call to conversion, and Lourdes offers the means to do that through Reconciliation, prayer, and spiritual counseling.

"In the Reconciliation Chapel," he continued, "people tell me they've come to Lourdes, but they really don't know why. They tell me that something inside them brought them here, an interior call much like Bernadette herself experienced. They find themselves in the Confession chapel, and again, they don't know why. When I start talking with them, however, I discover it has been a while since they've been in their parish, and the experience in Lourdes helps them to get back into the ministry of the Church and the practice of their faith."

Father Griffin pointed out that we live in a world today where the mindset is that everything has to be perfect. "So, when there is a problem, people say to themselves, let's go to Lourdes and be cured. I don't have a problem with that, but perhaps they need to ask themselves what does being cured mean? I think it means being healed, being able to accept the situation, to accept the imperfect, and to accept our own mortality. To me, a miracle is simply a physical experience of God's love in our lives."

At Lourdes, the Irish chaplain told me, people realize how fragile human nature is. The number of sick pilgrims at the Sanctuary can be quite overwhelming for some people. Witnessing how they are tended to by so many caring volunteers touches them in a deep and personal way. This in itself is a visible miracle at Lourdes. But there is another type of illness that is less visible. Chaplains at Lourdes continually meet with people who are mentally and emotionally wounded from past and present situations. "They are trying to do something about their lives and find some sort of inner peace," he says. "Many of them find it here."

Father Griffin says that when you look at the Lourdes experience, there is a great parallel between the Gospel and the apparitions. Christ called His disciples to Him; He prayed with them and He taught them. He revealed his divinity in the Transfiguration and then told His disciples to go out and teach all nations. The Virgin Mary did much the same thing with Bernadette. She prayed with her, instructed her to pray for sinners, revealed her heavenly identity, and then gave Bernadette a mission: to tell the priests (the Church) that she desired a chapel and for people to come in procession.

This, like Christ's mission, is for all of us. We have all been invited to pray, to convert, to be in community, and to enter into the "other" world where the Lady promised Bernadette happiness. What exactly is this "other" world? At the time of the apparitions, many were quick to interpret this as a reference to eternal life in heaven. It seemed that Bernadette's destiny was secured. But for the visionary, the "other" world held a deeper spiritual meaning. Father Griffin elaborates. "The 'other' world is the world of the Resurrection. We live in the current world, surrounded by its secularity, but as Christians we believe that the past is present here. In other words, we can see the face of Christ in the people and events around us. We are called to see beyond the secularity into the religious side, and in that way it is bringing the world of the Resurrection into our world today. Thus, we are able to live in our current world, but at the same time our minds are set and fixed on the spiritual side of things, and not just on the material."

Father Duguay's perspective on this is that "the 'other' world is the one Bernadette encountered in the grotto, the spiritual world, the world of the heart tied to God. She was immeasurably happy in the presence of the Lady. Even after the apparitions were over, the grotto would always hold special significance and happiness for her because of what she had experienced there. As a chaplain, I personally invite pilgrims who come to Lourdes to give themselves a chance to enter into this 'other' world, even if they don't understand all of it. I encourage them to be open and be empty. Inevitably, they will find themselves caught in it, not like a prisoner, but like a truly free person. You see, nothing is imposed here. Everything is an invitation. As the Lady said, 'Would you be kind enough to come here…?' I tell those in formation at the Hospitality that they, like Bernadette, have been called mysteriously to the grotto for a week, for two weeks, to facilitate a pilgrimage of people who could otherwise not make one. They, like Bernadette, have said *yes*. In doing this, they are entering the 'other' world."

The discussion of the "other" world would not be complete without the perspectives of Father Régis-Marie de La Teyssonnière, a man regarded by many as one of the world's leading authorities on Bernadette and her apparitions. He reflects, "There is the world of hate, violence, and suffering unto death, and the world of love, the gift of one's whole life. The Cross of Jesus separates the two. Bernadette learned this from the Holy Virgin at the first apparition when she received from her, with the Sign of the Cross, the secret of how to enter into the 'other' world. By his humility, Jesus brought us into touch with the 'other' world, the Kingdom of Heaven, where one lives in total love, in the total giving of oneself, and a total acceptance of the other. The 'other' world is the world of the Resurrection, the world of Christ, the world of the Holy Spirit, and the world of God, Our Father. It is a world of love and joy in spite of suffering. Even in pain and suffering Bernadette was always happy."

One cannot enter the world of Christ without entering in some degree into His passion. Although Bernadette certainly did this through her holy death, she also entered into the passion during the time of her apparitions. As God the Father humbled Himself to become man, Bernadette crawled on her knees and kissed the ground in penance. As our Jewish elder brothers ate bitter herbs with their Passover Meal to memorialize the suffering of their people, Bernadette ate the wild plants growing in the cave. As the prophet Isaiah foretold of man whose face would become disfigured and no longer human because of his suffering, Bernadette's face was transfigured by the mud of the spring. As Christ was stripped of His garments, Bernadette removed her shawl during the eighth and ninth apparitions, and her whole life would become a stripping of herself in order to clothe herself in Christ. Finally, as Christ's passion led to the Resurrection, Bernadette's penance led to the miraculous spring. At the heart of the message of Lourdes, therefore, through true spiritual conversion, new life awaits us all.

PART III
CHARITY

9.

VOLUNTEERISM

Volunteerism, the act of giving one's time, money, and labor freely to serve another fellow human being, is a fundamental concept in Christianity. Jesus Christ devoted His public ministry to teaching people the important news of loving and serving one another. In parable after parable, He illustrated this point, perhaps most memorably with the story of the Good Samaritan. Then, before He died, the Lord summarized His entire mission for His apostles at the Last Supper by washing their feet and declaring, *"For I have set you an example that you also should do as I have done to you"* (John 13:15).

To be a true disciple of Jesus, Christians are called to look for similar opportunities to serve their fellow humanity. Great saints throughout history have recognized and applied this truth, from St. Vincent de Paul to Mother Teresa. The Blessed Mother herself epitomized the act of service with words that would change salvation history, *"Here I am, the servant of the Lord; let it be with me according to your word"* (Luke 1:37). With this singular act of volunteerism, the lowly handmaid of the Lord prepared the way of redemption for the entire world through her Son, Jesus Christ.

The act of serving another human being is as fundamental a concept to Lourdes as it is to Christianity. It is fair to consider Bernadette Soubirous the first official volunteer at Lourdes, as she was the first to place herself willingly at the service of the Lady in the grotto. She gave freely of the one thing she had to offer—her time—with a promise to return for fifteen days, although she had no idea what this commitment would entail. From the earliest days of her apparitions, she shouldered the responsibility to pray and do penance for all sinners. This attitude of service and humility did not end with the apparitions; it followed her throughout her life and her vocation in tending the sick at the hospice and in the infirmary at Nevers. "When you are taking care of a sick person," she would instruct the novices, "you must withdraw before getting any thanks….The honor of caring for them is sufficient recompense for us."[1]

The honor of welcoming and caring for all those with special needs has been a privilege at Lourdes since the Sanctuary's earliest days. At first, it was the inhabitants of the town that took on the responsibility of helping visitors who needed assistance. As the shrine developed, the Garaison Fathers managed this responsibility until the volume of pilgrims in need required the formation of a special Confraternity of Hospitality, which remains in existence today under the title Hospitality of Our Lady of Lourdes. This unique organization consists of approximately eight thousand hospitality volunteers who come to serve at the shrine from all corners of the world. The commitment of these volunteers is to welcome all pilgrims (especially those with illness and disability), to facilitate their pilgrimage, and to promulgate the message of Lourdes, particularly through their acts of service. Between the months of April and October, it is estimated that the Sanctuary hosts more than seventy thousand people with special needs. An additional hundred thousand volunteers accompany these pilgrims from diocesan, national, or international hospitality organizations. An important function of the Hospitality of Our

Lady of Lourdes, the "welcoming" hospitality, is to coordinate efforts with these "accompanying" hospitality members.

To become a permanent member of the Hospitality of Our Lady of Lourdes, volunteers must undergo special training. The process of formation entails four annual visits to the Sanctuary, lasting from six to ten days each. Each *stagiaire*, or volunteer in training, must be at least eighteen years old and fully responsible for all his or her travel and lodging expenses. Antoine Tierny, president of the Hospitality of Our Lady of Lourdes, describes the special individuals that return year after year to serve the pilgrims visiting the Sanctuary:

> They pay their own travel costs, accommodation, and food to provide this service. They fulfill a triple mission: Firstly that of welcome, which is a key word. We welcome the pilgrims, and in particular the sick or [those with disabilities]. The second part of the mission is to assist with the great ceremonies, to make them accessible to all those pilgrims present. The third part of the mission is the transmission of the message of Lourdes; and to transmit it, you must know it. This is why we offer a formation over the first four years before the permanent engagement in the Hospitality.[2]

The highly visible members of the Hospitality, in their navy blue vests, can be found in and around the Sanctuary. They are present at the Tarbes-Lourdes Airport and the Lourdes Railway Station as a first line of welcome for pilgrims with illness and disability. With special transfer devices, the volunteers see that the pilgrims are properly and respectfully boarded onto buses and vans that will take them to the shrine. Upon their arrival, additional volunteers are prepared to take the pilgrims to their special place of accommodation called an *accueil*, a French word that means welcome. There are two *accueils* within the Domain, and a third one just outside the Sanctuary run by an Italian hospitality organization. A cross between an assisted-living center and a hotel, the *accueils* provide hospital beds, medical equipment, and special dietary needs for the seriously ill or for pilgrims with disabilities in an atmosphere of charity and prayer. The Accueil Notre Dame is a modern nine-hundred-bed facility run by the Sanctuary, while the Accueil Marie Saint Frai offers four hundred beds and is managed by a religious community. Pilgrims with less serious conditions are invited to stay in the numerous hotels surrounding the Domain.

One will also see Hospitality of Our Lady of Lourdes volunteers out and about on the Sanctuary grounds. They work in the holy places, they provide information to visitors, they push stretchers and wheelchairs and special hooded three-wheeled vehicles called chariots, they assist pilgrims in the baths, they sew vestments for the ceremonies, and they serve any other needs that may arise.

Father Patrick-Louis Desprez is the general chaplain to the Hospitality of Our Lady of Lourdes. He shared with me his responsibility at the Sanctuary. "As general chaplain to the Hospitality of Our Lady of Lourdes, I have received a mission from the bishop to be a religious presence in a lay association. The presence of a chaplain is to ensure that the message of Lourdes will be respected by all members of the Hospitality."

He explained that it is in the first year of formation that the hospitality volunteer discovers the message of Lourdes in the person of Bernadette, in the words Our Lady spoke, and in the reality of what the Sanctuary is today. The second year is focused on addressing the harmony that exists between the two different kinds of hospitalities, the one that accompanies and the one that welcomes. In the third year, the volunteers reflect on the reality of suffering and also on the dignity of the human person. In the fourth year, the mission is to broaden the attitude of the hospitality members to serve not only at Lourdes, but beyond. "We invite members to look into their own homes and communities to see where they can be of service," the general chaplain told me. "Lourdes is a place of knowledge that teaches people how to service their diocese."

Father Desprez observes that the number of hospitality volunteers accompanying pilgrimages to Lourdes is growing and transforming. Currently, there are over 230 accompanying hospitalities that come to the Sanctuary. While most of the hospitality volunteers come from western Europe, new groups have been arriving from Romania, Poland, and other places in eastern Europe, as well as from Asia. He acknowledges with particular interest the increasing presence of American volunteers at the shrine. The general chaplain believes that the increase in volunteerism at Lourdes stems from the desire to convert, to go from one's own personal self to a giving of self.

What would motivate thousands of people from around the world each year to willingly give a week or more of their vacations to serve at Lourdes? Perhaps the volunteers themselves provide the best answer. Philippe Tardy-Joubert comes from a family that has served at Lourdes for five generations. When he sat down to speak with me, he was celebrating fifty years of volunteerism with the Hospitality of Our Lady of Lourdes. For Philippe, volunteerism has always been a family affair. "My grandmother was a member of the Hospitality, my father was, I am, my children are, and my grandchildren are. When I was young, my parents went to Lourdes with all of their children, not just for themselves, but to pray and serve others. This was a part of our education. I am very blessed to witness the importance of Lourdes in my parents' lives, and to discover the values of the Gospel with my family. I invite present members of the Hospitality to come with their children and grandchildren. Young people are particularly geared for volunteerism at Lourdes because of the physical nature of many of the services performed here."

For five decades, Philippe has served the Hospitality in all possible capacities. Most recently, he has been appointed as coordinator of the International Conference of Hospitaliers of Our Lady of Lourdes. In this capacity, he can appreciate the diverse profile and motivations of a Lourdes hospitality member. "Some volunteers first came to Lourdes with their families, like me, when they were very young. Others came when they were older. Some already exhibited a strong commitment to the Church and an involvement in helping [the sick and those with disabilities]. Others have decided to become involved where they live, after having experienced the Lourdes service first. Some were motivated to serve as hospitality members because they have sick people among their close family or friends. We also see how many have been able to face their own health problems more easily because of the service they have provided at the Sanctuary.

"The sick are for us the image of Christ suffering," Philippe continued. "We must be for them the image of the compassionate Christ. As hospitality members, we must see that all people are regarded with great respect, whatever their [limitations] or form of poverty. After our experience in Lourdes, when we are back in our parishes or in our normal environment, we can no longer be indifferent to the integration of the weakest members of the community. Our mission is to live and spread the Gospel. The goal is not to change your lives for five days a year, but to change your lives forever. We are happy to be pilgrims and to be servants in this place, at the invitation of the Queen of Heaven."

John Howard is another long-term volunteer at Lourdes. He first went to the Sanctuary as a fourteen-year-old in 1966. He was selected as one of six parishioners from his parish in London to make the pilgrimage due to a condition of being semiparaplegic, or "spastic," from birth. It was his first experience being away from home. As John recalls, the first miracle he experienced in Lourdes was his own self-revelation. "When you are born sick, you often have the opinion you are the only sick person in the world. In Lourdes, my eyes were opened. When I went to the Domain, I saw people a lot sicker than me. There were little babies there, all the way up to people in their nineties. I realized I wasn't the only person in my situation. In fact, I was very fortunate. I could walk, I could talk, and I could pick things up. I felt grateful for my blessings. Four years later, I was selected again to go to Lourdes. But this time the organizers put me down as one of the helpers. I didn't think I could do that job because of my disability, but they assured me I would be assigned light duties. And so I agreed and went as a volunteer. It's been so rewarding, I've been going back every year for the last thirty-six years."

Some volunteers have made their mark in just a few short years. Take Marlene Watkins, for example, a familiar face at Lourdes. She is the founder and volunteer executive director of Our Lady of Lourdes Hospitality North American Volunteers, a nonprofit 501(c)3 charity with a threefold purpose: first, to share the Gospel message of Lourdes as given by Our Lady in the grotto to Bernadette, calling us to prayer, conversion, penance, and procession;

second, to invite others to the privilege of serving the universal Church at Lourdes, providing greatly needed English-speaking volunteers in various capacities at the Sanctuary; and third, to accommodate and care for special needs pilgrims traveling from North America to Lourdes who would not be able to travel to Lourdes without assistance. The mission of the apostolate is "to extend the invitation of Mary the Mother of God to serve the sick and suffering at Lourdes and at home, as exemplified by St. Bernadette in humility, obedience, and simplicity."

Marlene's personal introduction to Lourdes and the graces she received there was, for her, nothing short of a miracle. Her first pilgrimage occurred in the year 2000 when a friend of more than thirty years had her business card plucked out of a fishbowl at work and won two tickets to Europe. She immediately invited Marlene. In truth, accepting the free airfare had little to do with Lourdes, as Marlene did not know much about Bernadette and the apparitions at the time. Her main motivation to go was to see the Holy Father, Pope John Paul II, whom she deeply admired. The two women decided to make the trip a once-in-a-lifetime experience, and so they planned excursions to several holy places, including Fatima, Rome, and a small town in France called Nevers. Marlene's friend had read a book on the incorruptible saints and wanted to visit the body of St. Bernadette. Marlene agreed to go, although she had no interest in such things whatsoever.

The experience in Lourdes was particularly powerful for Marlene, with the *piscines* being one of the highpoints of her pilgrimage. Not really knowing what to expect, she waited on line a few hours before it was her turn to enter the baths. When it was over, Marlene had an overwhelming sense of peace, something long missing in her life. She recognized at once that something inexplicable had happened and that she had experienced deep healing and deepening conversion. She returned home filled with profound gratitude for the experience. There was no thought in her mind, however, that she would ever return to Lourdes or Europe again. Therefore, she was quite surprised to find herself on the same line for the baths exactly one year later.

On this occasion, she had come to the Sanctuary with two seriously ill loved ones. The situation seemed desperate, and Lourdes was the only recourse these women had for hope and support. This time, instead of waiting for hours to get into the baths, the three Americans waited for four days. The lines were enormous and seemed to grow longer each day. The fourth day was Ascension Thursday, 2001, a day that would set a new shrine record for the number of women bathed. Concerned that her companions would not get in, Marlene sacrificed her place in line to someone else to speak with a badge-bearing man behind the gate. She proceeded to beg him in her rusty high school French to let her relatives in, as they greatly needed healing and had come so far and had waited so long. The man could not understand her because he did not speak French; he quickly enlisted the assistance of an English bath attendant. The conversation quickly turned, and the female bath matron asked Marlene if she could touch her toes. Without thinking or asking her why, Marlene demonstrated that she could. Unbeknown to Marlene at the time, the woman was testing her to see if she was physically fit and if she would do what she was told without hesitation. Pleased at the response, the woman looked into Marlene's eyes and said, "Come with me this day to bathe the sick and dying, and I give you my word those you love will come in."

Marlene ran over and told the ladies to stay in line; she was going into the baths to help, and she would in essence pull them through from the other side. She went inside the gates where a woman tied an apron around her waist, and she was given a number. From there she was assigned to *Piscine* 4, where she discovered to her dismay a group of Italian women who did not speak English or French. Devoid of a common language, communication was reduced to pointing and gestures, which at times became rather brisk. The passionate Italians were frustrated that the American helper did not seem to know what she was doing. They did not like how Marlene wrung out the towels, making the floor slippery and dangerous, or more importantly, the appearance of her lack of understanding that this was precious Lourdes water. They corrected her mistakes, pushing their fists firmly in the small of her back and pulling her shoulder blades together sharply to correct her posture and protect her back while lifting the sick.

Despite the physical demands of the day, Marlene was awed and humbled to witness the deep and personal effects the baths had on the women who passed through *Piscine* 4. As a mother of five sons and a recent grandmother, she had seen a lot of things in her life, but what she witnessed on this particular day was extraordinary. It would become one of the most privileged days of her life. She was further overjoyed at the opportunity to assist both loved ones whom she had brought from New York, each of whom experienced wonderful spiritual conversions during their baths. The odds of both of these women coming through her *piscine* was unlikely, and she realized that this, too, was a special gift and blessing. Marlene observed an important need in the baths that day. While her English was useless to her *piscine* partners, it was extremely valuable for communicating with the pilgrims that had come to be bathed. Half of the women she had served that day spoke English as a primary or secondary language, and Marlene was able to welcome, assist, and comfort them.

At the conclusion of the volunteer service, Marlene repeated the prayer ritual offered at the beginning of the shift. She prayed, made the Sign of the Cross, and knelt down to kiss the floor. As she knelt down, she had a feeling of fullness in her chest, and as her lips touched the floor, she made an impromptu promise to Our Lady that she would return to help in one year's time and bring ten good Catholic American women with her. Since she was still unaware that the people working at the baths were volunteers and not paid employees, her promise to Our Lady to bring American volunteers to Lourdes was as remarkable to her as it was spontaneous. Therefore, she concluded afterward that God must have put this intention in her heart.

A woman wearing a badge with several flags indicating the languages she could speak happened to come by at the end of the service. Marlene confirmed that the woman could translate a message to the Italian women for her before they departed. "Tell these ladies that I thank them for all they showed me," she instructed the translator. "I'm very grateful. And please ask them to forgive me for all the mistakes I made." The multilingual woman said she would relay the message. The Italian ladies reminded Marlene not to forget to wear her badge the next time. She told them she didn't have a badge; she wasn't an employee. When she explained how she ended up working in the baths, the translator was astonished. This was quite unheard of. To volunteer at Lourdes, a person needed a letter from a priest; there was training involved, and a commitment of at least a week. When the woman relayed Marlene's message and situation to the Italians, they rushed upon her, kissing her and lovingly embracing her with gratitude. They asked her if she had had an opportunity to experience a bath herself on her pilgrimage. Since she hadn't, they reopened the *piscine* and helped her into the bath. She had no time to spiritually prepare at the moment. Silently, Marlene asked God to grant her the greatest grace that she was in need of as she approached the bath. The moment her feet hit the water, she had yet another life-changing experience. The grace was so powerful, unexpected, and *freeing* that she knew it had come from God. It was a continuation of what had began in the baths for her a year earlier…conversion and healing grace.

Marlene returned home and spoke to her husband, Bill, immediately about her promise to bring American women to help in the baths. He was very supportive of the idea. Turning her promise into a plan, however, was another matter altogether. The fact was that in those days, American volunteers at Lourdes were a rarity. Only about thirty volunteers of the total eight thousand from around the world were from the United States. The country had not played a role in the development of pilgrimage to Lourdes in the mid-1800s, because at that time an American would have had to travel a month by steamship across the ocean to serve one week at the Sanctuary. It simply wasn't practical. With the advent of flight and the influx of English-speaking pilgrims from Asia, Africa, the Middle East, and other parts of the world pouring into Lourdes, the need—and the means to respond—were now in place.

After writing several requests to Lourdes for permission to bring American volunteers, Marlene finally received a response. She returned the following May with ten women, one man, and a Canadian priest under the name "North American Volunteers." It was an exhausting but rewarding week of service. During the week, Mr. Gabriel Barbry, the then president of Our Lady of Lourdes Hospitality, summoned Marlene. He instructed her to bring more Americans to Lourdes. "I told him in my terrible French that they were not talking to the best person. What they needed was an important woman with a lot of money and a lot of influence, someone who knew bishops, and someone prestigious and known," Marlene remembers. "I insisted that I was just a housewife. How could I possibly do what they were asking?" When the president and his French volunteer organizers finally understood what she was saying, they reminded her of the story of Bernadette Soubirous. "Go back and get some more American women. Come back in May, June, in September and October, and we need lots of men as well." They wouldn't let her leave until she hesitantly agreed, consoling herself that with God all things are possible.

On July 16, 2002, Marlene and five others formally founded Our Lady of Lourdes Hospitality North American Volunteers. They drafted a mission statement and organized a board of directors consisting of laypeople, medical professionals, and a Catholic priest. Marlene and Bill sought and received a private blessing from their bishop. The newly founded American apostolate quickly established friendships overseas. A series of speaking engagements both in the States and abroad together with word-of-mouth advertising enabled the organization to bring nine groups of American volunteers to Lourdes in 2003—165 people in total—to serve wherever they were needed. During one of these pilgrimages, Mr. Barbry once again called for Marlene. This time he had a written statement for her prepared in English that he had been practicing. "I know you for one year," he worded slowly, "and I see for one year that you are a fruit." Marlene smiled and thanked him for his well-meaning compliment. "And you are nothing and nobody," the president kindly continued. "Even though you have no means, all these people come. It's impossible for one woman to accomplish this. This must be the desire of Our Lady's heart and the hand of God." He followed this pronouncement with an invitation for Marlene to return to the United States and formally place the apostolate under the official authority of a bishop.

The Most Reverend James Moynihan of the Syracuse, New York, diocese did not really know Marlene Watkins in 2003. But he did have a strong Marian devotion and he had been to Lourdes. After again meeting with Marlene and Bill, the bishop agreed to observe the unique volunteer organization and their work for one year. Then, after an additional year of observation and prayerful consideration, he signed the papers elevating the first Lourdes hospitality in the Americas to a Public Association of the Christian Faithful in the Church on June 10, 2005.

During the first volunteer service, the apostolate recognized an additional calling: to provide travel and accommodations for special needs North Americans through customized pilgrimages to Lourdes. This was initiated in the fall of 2003. Another initiative with the U.S. military to draw dependents of military personnel stationed in Europe to serve at the Sanctuary began that summer, centered on involving the service of young people in preparation for the sacrament of Confirmation with their energy, strength, and talents. The following year, a special program was formulated with Franciscan University at Steubenville, Ohio, to invite Catholic college students to the service of the sick at Lourdes.

Since its inception, Marlene entrusted the ministry entirely to God, the one who called it into being in the first place. Her faith has been duly tested, beginning with the very first pilgrimage. At the time, Air France required a minimum of ten persons to qualify for group airfare. Two weeks before ticketing, two people needed to cancel. Marlene didn't want to let go of the seats because she knew she would lose her group status. Desperate, she added two names: Bernadette Soubirous and Thérèse (of Lisieux) Martin. And then she prayed. Sure enough, about a week later, two people she had never met called and said they had heard about a group of people going to Lourdes to help in the baths. Could they come? "I cancelled Bernadette and Thérèse immediately and substituted their names," Marlene laughs now. "This happened several times in the beginning. An agent at Air France told me how she felt bad that Bernadette and Thérèse never got to go to Lourdes. I assured the agent that Soubirous and Martin could go to Lourdes whenever they wanted."

Each year, the North American volunteer ministry grows, sending hundreds of men, women, and young people from the United States, Canada, Mexico, and the Caribbean Islands to serve or to be served in Lourdes. Each of these pilgrims has his or her own incredible story. "Many women would share, for example, how they'd had an abortion when they were young and how they felt like they had a hole inside them after that experience," Marlene relates. "They had been suffering terribly in silence. When they went into the water at Lourdes, though, it was as if a liquid grace finally filled that emptiness. Some would confide how they were physically or sexually abused, some tragically, when they were young or small. They were so wounded or cracked, fragile and barely held together throughout life's difficulties, and somehow the water at Lourdes filled those cracks and made them whole again. We've seen others bitter at God that he would abandon them in their suffering as little children, and then suddenly and surprisingly they would find healing so many years later. We would hear these stories week after week, and we knew something extraordinary was happening every day in those baths. At Lourdes, people were finding the healing, peace, and reconciliation that they were longing for and missing."

Witnessing the exuberance of people as they discover new life in Lourdes is a rewarding experience for all those who volunteer. Witnessing the peaceful acceptance of the end of life is equally rewarding. "People have come to Lourdes having been away from the sacraments," Marlene recounts. "They were often poisoned with bitterness. Through God's grace, they were spiritually healed at Lourdes and returned to the sacraments to die the most holy deaths. That was their miracle. And it's a profound miracle. We often encounter people who are not looking for a miracle at all, but with one simple wish: to die in great peace. And they get that. They get the gift and the grace and the courage. They die embracing God's will for them, and those are really sweet miracles. The truth is, we're all terminal. We're all going to die. We all are in exile, on a pilgrimage, created not to be here, but with God in eternity."

Our Lady of Lourdes Hospitality North American Volunteers has made impressive strides to increase awareness about the necessity and privilege of serving the universal Church in the holy shrine in the Pyrenees. But the apostolate knows there is still much work to be done. Nearly half of the six million people who pilgrimage to Lourdes each year speak English as their primary or secondary language. Yet only about 10 percent of the eight thousand volunteers that serve these pilgrims annually are from the combined English-speaking countries of Australia, Canada, Ireland, America, and the United Kingdom. More awareness and more help are needed. In an effort to invite ordinary people to experience the extraordinary, Marlene has spoken at conferences to thousands and on EWTN to millions.

Recognizing that not everyone who has a desire to go to Lourdes can actually do so, North American Lourdes Volunteers was inspired to bring Lourdes to those not able to travel on a pilgrimage journey. In October 2004, the apostolate launched the first Lourdes Virtual Pilgrimage. The purpose is to give audiences at parishes, hospitals, nursing homes, prisons, and schools the same tour of the Sanctuary that they would receive in person through the help of hundreds of images projected on a screen. The group begins the tour by stopping at the grotto to pray, allowing the "pilgrims" to offer their petitions in silence to Our Lady of Lourdes as images of people also praying in the grotto are displayed. A piece of the grotto rock entrusted to the association by the bishop of Lourdes is passed around so that people may touch it, just as they would do at Lourdes. Water brought from the spring is placed in a bowl on a pedestal, and people are invited to come up and wash some water on their faces, just as they do at the water taps at Lourdes. A priest, either local or one from the Sanctuary who may come to the United States to participate in the virtual pilgrimage tours, offers the Blessed Sacrament to give a eucharistic blessing to individuals and families who attend. The tour concludes with a mini-candlelight procession with candles from the grotto that are lighted as the people in attendance pray a decade of the Rosary together, just as they do at the end of the evening at Lourdes. In addition to the two-hour virtual tours, the apostolate has also begun providing weekend retreats and four-night parish missions.

"It is difficult to explain why people come to Lourdes to volunteer," says Gabriel Barbry, retired president of Our

Lady of Lourdes Hospitality, as he and I shared lunch together in the volunteers' cafeteria. "People can't always explain why they come here or why they serve. It's somewhere deep in their heart. Some people come just to work, and not so much to pray. Others come more to pray than to work. Some go to Mass every day, others not so often. Wherever the person is in their spiritual journey, we have to help them along. We welcome everybody. We can't leave anybody by the side."

Mr. Barbry says that most of the eight thousand hospitality volunteers come from France and Italy. They also come from other parts of Europe such as Spain, the British Isles, Germany, and the Netherlands. For the first time, volunteers are coming to Lourdes from Croatia, Poland, Romania, Australia, and Asia. "Every year, each country has a meeting of all the hospitalities in their country. Representatives from the Hospitality of Our Lady of Lourdes attend these meetings so we can talk about what's going on and look for ideas on how to improve things."

When I asked him what he saw as the vision for the future of volunteerism at the Sanctuary, he said it would always be first and foremost to spread the message of Lourdes. To him, that can be summarized as a strong conversion of prayer and of the Church throughout the world. "There is still a lot of work to do," he says, "but we are very motivated to send out this message of Lourdes. It is a message of peace, and therefore it has to come from the heart." Judging by the growth of volunteerism at Lourdes, it seems that the message is being received.

10.

THE HOLY FATHER VISITS

Pope John Paul II was well known to the world for his strong Marian devotion. He took as his apostolic motto *Totus Tuus*, a Latin prayer he borrowed from St. Louis de Montfort, meaning "totally yours." Since de Montfort had championed Marian devotion, the motto was a direct reference to the Blessed Mother. Having lost his own mother at a young age, the young Pole naturally turned to the Holy Virgin for guidance and protection throughout his life. As pope, he openly credited Our Lady of Fatima as sparing him from the bullet of would-be assassin Mehmet Ali Agca on May 13, 1981, the feast day of the apparitions of Fatima. A year later the pontiff traveled to Portugal in thanksgiving for his life, placing the bullet that had been removed from his shoulder at the feet of the Virgin.

It was the assassination attempt that prevented Pope John Paul II from presiding over the closing session of the Eucharistic Congress held in Lourdes in July of 1981. While he had been to Lourdes in 1947 as a young priest, it was his desire to visit the grotto of Massabielle during his papacy. This dream would not be frustrated for long. On August 15, 1983, Lourdes received its first papal pilgrim, as Pope John Paul II knelt in prayer at the same place Bernadette prayed 125 years before. He came simply as a pilgrim during the Holy Year of the Redemption. Before leaving France, he imparted the following words to the prime minister. "I am happy to have, finally, added Lourdes to the chain of Marian sanctuaries that I have visited around the world to pray with fellow Christians. It is a basic devotion in my life and I would like to train the Church in prayer, in Marian Devotion. Prayer is the first task and call of the pope; it is the first condition of my service in the Church and in the world. It was good that I, too, was able to kneel in front of the grotto of Massabielle and be a pilgrim in Lourdes."[1]

On May 13, 1992, the eleventh anniversary of the assassination attempt, Pope John Paul II announced to the world the institution of a World Day of the Sick. He chose February 11, the feast of Our Lady of Lourdes, as the date on which this occasion would be celebrated throughout the world. The first World Day of the Sick took place fittingly enough at Lourdes the following year, 1993, with the theme that the sick and people with disabilities will have their rightful place in society and in the Church. Each year thereafter, the celebration has traveled to different continents to build worldwide awareness about those whom Jesus loved in a special way: the sick and the suffering.

Meanwhile, in Vatican City, Pope John Paul II started a tradition that is still honored today. Each year on February 11 a papal Mass is held for the sick in St. Peter's Basilica. Patients in wheelchairs and on gurneys are strategically placed around the high altar. At the end of the service, the basilica lights are dimmed. Then, thousands of candles are lit inside red and orange tulip-shaped containers and held high as the Lourdes hymn [included in the appendix] is sung in various languages. The Holy Father, explaining why the World Day of the Sick is observed on the feast of Our Lady of Lourdes, said Christians are called to "entrust themselves to Christ and to his heavenly mother, who never abandon those who turn to them in times of pain and trial."[2]

The twelfth annual World Day of the Sick returned to Lourdes in 2004 in commemoration of the 150th anniversary of the dogma of the Immaculate Conception. That summer, three hundred thousand people were present in the Sanctuary on August 14 and 15 when Pope John Paul II returned to Lourdes a second time to mark this important occasion. It was the 104th foreign voyage of his pontificate and the last one he would make on this earth. This time, the pope was a stark contrast to the energetic man in white who had made the same journey in 1983. He now arrived in a wheelchair, crippled by age and the advanced symptoms of Parkinson's disease. He came, he explained in words weak and breathless, "to unite myself with the millions of pilgrims who converge on Lourdes every year, to ask for the help and intercession of the Virgin Mary."[3]

Dr. Theillier recalled fondly the pope's second visit to Lourdes. "For him, this was a very important place. The best proof of this is the fact that he wanted to come here before he died. I remember the moment when the Holy Father got off the popemobile and knelt on the kneeler—he very nearly fell over. Some thought that it was due to his weakness or his illness...yet in fact he was greatly moved emotionally."[4]

Father Duguay was also privileged to welcome the pontiff to Lourdes in 2004. He remembered that the pope wanted to go to the grotto first like any pilgrim, to make the Sign of the Cross and pray. "I was only a few feet away from him. He was in a wheelchair, and then, briefly, he stood up. I never thought he would be able to. To me, it looked as though he had the weight of the world on his shoulders, in addition to his own illness. What struck me most was when he said, 'Kneeling here at the Grotto of Massabielle, I am moved by the feeling that I have arrived at the destination of my pilgrimage.' At one point in his private prayer, his head dropped down to his chest. From behind, all we could see were his shoulders. Literally, he had collapsed. I thought perhaps he had expired. I'm sure the whole thing lasted only a few moments, but to us it seemed much longer. The cardinals surrounding him respectfully allowed the Holy Father to experience this moment. Then they held him up and gave him some water from the spring, which he drank. It was very, very emotional."

Among the French clergy that day was the former vicar and Hospitality chaplain of Lourdes, Father Régis-Marie de La Teyssonnière. A man who had grown up in Pau, a city no more than thirty miles from Lourdes, the events in the grotto at Massabielle in 1858 permanently shaped his Catholicism and his priesthood. The papal visit to Lourdes in 2004 was the third time the chaplain would have the opportunity to greet the pontiff in person. "It was an incredible joy after months of preparation to welcome the Holy Father to Lourdes. We had erected an enormous television screen for the event and we watched excitedly as his car drove through the streets of Lourdes. Then, suddenly, it pulled up right in front of us and he emerged as happy to see us as we were to see him. He was wheeled immediately to the front of the grotto to pray. Once there, two bishops gently helped the pontiff to his knees. As I watched his face, I saw him begin to cry—imagine, the Holy Father, crying in front of the grotto. It was so beautiful and sorrowful. I thought for a moment that he was dying. It was an incredible experience. Then the bishops helped him to sit down again. He was very, very sick. It was only with much difficulty that he drank the water of the spring."

The rector, Father Zambelli, was the one who offered the water to the pope. "When I was a child," he reflected, "I used to envy people who in their lifetime had the opportunity to meet a saint, to listen to him, and to see him praying. I received this grace at Lourdes in welcoming Pope John Paul II. Approaching him and giving him a glass of fresh water as a sign of hospitality, I knew that I was giving to him the best gift: the water of the spring that the Virgin Mary asked Bernadette to find inside the grotto. This spring is, in fact, the permanent sign she gave to us of her presence. In its transparency, fluidity, freshness, clearness, the water of the grotto reflects the soul of the Virgin Mary. To drink this water means to fill oneself with her love, her kindness, her purity, and her strength. These are the feelings I had when I offered the glass to the Holy Father."

During his visit, the pope presented a rare papal honor, the golden rose, to the Lourdes shrine as a lasting sign of his dedication. After staying a night at the Accueil Notre Dame guesthouse, he led the Rosary reflections during the torchlight procession and presided over Mass on the feast of the Assumption of Mary, the day that draws the greatest number of pilgrims to Lourdes each year. Joining him on the altar were a thousand priests, a hundred bishops, and fifteen cardinals. Several members of the civil authorities were also in attendance to celebrate the occasion.

Father Duguay remembered vividly the procession that day on August 15. It was as if he were watching the Church being formed before his eyes. But this church was not made of granite or wood—it was made of 250,000 living people. "Christ, we know, is the cornerstone of the Church," Father Duguay explained. "Mary is the first stone because she gave us that cornerstone. Therefore, we follow Mary in procession because she leads us and takes us with her. That day, she was followed by Pope John Paul II, the head of the Church. After him came the faithful from all over the world—Europe,

Australia, Canada, China, Japan, and Hong Kong—all living stones united with the cornerstone. This is the Church Our Lady asked for, because the Church is a living community. The pope that day, on the great feast of Our Lady, was inviting people to build it with him, and they responded, singing with joy. It was the most beautiful experience I have ever had."

Another emotional moment for Father Duguay occurred as the pontiff made one final stop at the grotto to pray before leaving the Sanctuary. The chaplain had been hearing confessions at the Chapel of Reconciliation during this time. When he emerged from the chapel, he was struck by the tremendous silence that had settled over the Domain. Despite the extraordinary number of people present at the shrine, there was silence everywhere. It seemed as though the whole Church was praying in unity with the Holy Father. Father Duguay could not see the small figure in white, but he knew when the pope's prayer was over, because he could hear the crowds yelling, "*Viva il Papa!*"

From his summer residence of Castel Gondolfo three days later, Pope John Paul II recalled fond memories in his general audience about his recent visit to what he referred to as the "sanctuary of human suffering." He said,

> I would like to thank God who, in his goodness, allowed me to make a pilgrimage to Lourdes. I thank the Blessed Virgin for the atmosphere of deep prayer and meditation of this encounter. I remember with emotion the immense crowd of pilgrims present there, especially the sick who were in pride of place and who had come to seek comfort and hope through the Blessed Virgin Mary. I hope that all the young people present will take away with them memories of this pilgrimage

that will help them to become men and women of freedom in Christ![5]

For Father de La Teyssonnière, Pope John Paul II's second visit to Lourdes was a "Bernadette experience." He explained: "For Bernadette, the eighteen apparitions followed the Mysteries of the Rosary. She was joyful at seeing the Lady during the first seven apparitions. In the next four, she began to suffer in accordance with the messages. During the last seven apparitions, Bernadette's joy returned, ending with a glorious appearance of the Holy Virgin in which she never looked more beautiful. In the same way, the Holy Father demonstrated a similar pattern. When he arrived at Lourdes, he was joyful, but a joy that would only last a short time. Once he entered the sanctuary of the grotto, he also entered into a deep and incredible suffering, obvious to all. Before he left Lourdes, we chaplains had the privilege of meeting the Holy Father. We entered the room one by one and kissed his ring, imparting a brief word to him. He did not respond verbally, but his face was literally shining with peace and joy. It was for him, and for us all, a glorious mystery."

Father de La Teyssonnière recalled the last half-hour of the pope's visit as he prayed in the grotto, surrounded by people in wheelchairs and on gurneys. The great silence while the Holy Father prayed was not unlike the great silence that was said to have taken place while Bernadette was in ecstasy. Those in attendance in 1858 must have strained to catch a glimpse at the remarkable expression on Bernadette's face, much the way they gazed now in wonder at the Holy Father, whose face was projected through technology not just to the hundreds of thousands in the Sanctuary that day, but to millions of viewers around the world.

While most everyone present for the pope's visit to Lourdes was profoundly affected, some were touched more deeply than others. One such person was Linda de Plazaola, a young mother of two originally from Marseilles, France. Twenty years prior, she had been involved in a serious car accident in which she suffered injury to her spine. As a result, she was forced to wear a corset and experienced terrible migraines every couple of days. In order to sleep, she had to take painkillers and adjust her pillow in a certain way so as to minimize the pain. Linda came to Lourdes to see the pontiff. At the moment she heard him say, "I bless you...." to the crowd, she felt her illness disappear. That evening, for the first time in twenty years, she fell asleep without any painkillers and without the need to adjust her pillow. On August 17, two days after the Holy Father's visit, she went to the Medical Bureau and announced that she had been made well. The event was so powerful for her, she has become a regular volunteer, helping with the sick at Lourdes.

"Since then I have felt the need to be at the service of the sick and I have returned to Lourdes...as a hospitality member with the Rosary Pilgrimage. I then got involved in a team teaching catechism. I try to explain what I have understood in the message of Christ: 'Love one another,' for in my heart I have the proof of the love of God. Even if no medical examination can prove the disappearance of my pain, I know in the depths of my heart, and I believe it is my duty to testify to the grace I received in Lourdes on August 15, 2004, thanks to John Paul II."[6]

Through his teachings and example during his twenty-seven-year pontificate, the legendary Pope John Paul II taught the world not only how to live in freedom, but also how to suffer and die with dignity. Never before was a pontiff more vulnerable before the world and the watchful eye of the media. His brave and powerful witness at the close of his life continues to give strength to those who come to Lourdes in much the same condition. At Lourdes, the dying are reminded to have patience with their suffering and to hold out for the promise of eternal life. They are also reminded of sin and its forgiveness, which they have in common with the healthy, and for whom they can offer up their suffering. This gives them purpose and strength. In our Catholic faith, suffering is redemptive and for many, indispensable for their sanctity. The afflicted, the sick, and the dying who are not physically cured at Lourdes are still offered a profound opportunity to conform to the will of God and offer up their suffering. This, as the Holy Father exhibited, is a great lesson and reward of Lourdes.

11.

LOURDES, TODAY AND TOMORROW

The Sanctuary of Lourdes or "the Domain," as it is still referred to, sprawls today over 120 scenic acres of Pyrenees geography, couched in beauty by tree-covered foothills and the twisting river Gave. Within its boundaries exist three basilicas, one church, numerous chapels and other places of worship, a mile-long Way of the Cross, the grotto, the baths, two accommodation centers for the sick, the Medical Bureau, offices to distribute Lourdes water throughout the world, and the official bookstore. The acreage, the number of places of worship, and the impressive amount of pilgrims—some two hundred million in total from more than 170 countries—make Lourdes the most popular Marian shrine in Europe and one of the largest holy places in the world.

While visitors can be found at Lourdes any time of year, the traditional pilgrimage season opens with Holy Week in the spring and lasts through the end of October. This is the time that the daily processions, international Masses, and other large ceremonies take place. At the height of the pilgrimage season there is an average of fifty Masses celebrated in various languages in the Sanctuary each day. The day that continues to attract the greatest number of pilgrims each year is August 15, the feast of the Assumption of Mary. Other important off-season dates are February 11, the feast of Our Lady of Lourdes; February 18, the feast of Bernadette; and December 8, the feast of the Immaculate Conception.

The grotto of Massabielle where Bernadette's apparitions took place in 1858 is considered to be the heart of the Sanctuary. The iron grille that once stretched across the front of the cave was removed prior to the centenary of the apparitions and was later installed in a replica of the grotto in the Vatican Gardens. This allows pilgrims to freely enter into the recesses of the rock where they can view the source of the spring that Bernadette uncovered. Gone also are the numerous crutches that once decorated the walls, symbolizing past cures. Today the stone face of the grotto has become blackened and worn smooth by the touch of hands, lips, and rosaries passed lovingly and reverently over it for so many years. In the ivy-framed niche overhead, Fabisch's famous Madonna still adorns the rock, marking the place and moment in which the Immaculate Conception revealed her identity. At night the statue is lit from behind and further illuminated by a large candelabra directly below to symbolize the prayers of the faithful. A simple stone altar has been installed for Mass, and an adjacent receptacle accepts written prayer petitions from pilgrims passing through.

The Savy millstream has long been piped underground to the Gave to increase the walking area between the grotto and the river. Actually, the river itself has twice been diverted from its original course and today runs several meters away from the grotto to make room for the large numbers of pilgrims. Simple metal benches stand in neat rows on the pavement before the cave, and a small paving stone marks the location from which Bernadette gazed upon the Lady during her first apparition. Also channeled underground is the miraculous spring. Its source of clear running water may be viewed beneath lighted glass panels in the cave's recesses, when bouquets of flowers left by pilgrims do not obscure it. The spring continues to pump some 27,000 gallons of water a day since the early days of its discovery, even in times of drought. From the grotto, the water is routed beneath the pavement to a reservoir that supplies the baths and thirty-five fountains that pilgrims can use for drinking, washing, and collecting water.

The water of Lourdes is a sign of a greater water: the water of Baptism. To wash recalls the sacrament of Baptism in which our sins are washed away and we become children of God. It is because of our need to be reborn, forgiven, purified, and reconciled that we come to this water. The water of Lourdes should not, however, be confused with holy water. It is the faith of the people that makes it special. Bernadette advised others to take the water like a medicine. "But you must have faith, you must pray," she said. "This water is of no use without faith!"[1] The popularity of the water of the spring comes from the miracles attributed to it. Forty-nine of the sixty-seven Church-declared miracles occurred through contact with this water, whether by applying it, drinking it, or bathing in it.

Nearly half a million pilgrims visit the marble-clad baths or *piscines* each year, and for many it is a deeply moving experience and the highlight of their pilgrimage. Truly, the baths are a place of prayer. Since 1954, the baths have been located inside low stone buildings set against the hillside just beyond the grotto. There are nineteen separate baths, seventeen for adults and two for children. Hundreds of people are bathed in these waters daily. For the long lines of people that form each day to take advantage of the healing waters, there is some covered seating available. Leaflets are available in many languages to explain the process and meaning of bathing in the spring at Lourdes. The baths are open Monday through Saturday all year long from 9:00 to 11:00 a.m. and again from 2:00 to 4:00 p.m. On Sundays, they are open only in the afternoon. While people with illness and disability are a common sight at the baths, healthy pilgrims are also found among the ranks to bathe as mortification or for peace. Taking a bath at Lourdes challenges a person's need for comfort and dignity, but it is a certainly a visible and tangible demonstration of faith.

"To take off your clothes in front of other people isn't easy," explained Gabriel Barbry, who in his retirement from serving as president of the Hospitality of Our Lady of Lourdes was working in the service of the men's *piscines* the day I spoke with him. "In effect, you are laying yourself bare to the world. You are quite vulnerable at this moment. Working the baths, we see things we really don't understand. We see real life. We see a lot of people suffering. It is a great importance to see the sheer witness of people coming there. There are many tears. It is truly touching to see a strong man cry."

Situated between the baths and the grotto is an area where pilgrims may leave lighted candles as a part of their prayer offering. Candles have burned continuously in this area of the grotto since February 18, 1858, the date Bernadette brought the first one; millions of candles in all. Each year, over seven hundred tons of candles are burned for prayers of petitions and thanksgiving. The perpetual glow of the candles is also a symbol of Christ, who is the light of the world.

Dominating the Sanctuary of Lourdes are the Basilica of the Immaculate Conception and the Rosary Basilica, two grand houses of worship that are the most recognizable of all structures in the Domain. Together, they provide a backdrop to many of the important celebrations at Lourdes. The

Basilica of the Immaculate Conception, or Upper Basilica, is widely known for its ornate stained-glass windows. The windows of the side chapels tell the history of Lourdes from the first apparition to the crowning of the statue of Our Lady in 1876. The upper windows narrate the ongoing proclamation of the mystery of the Immaculate Conception from the beginning of the world until the dogma issued by Pius IX in 1854. There are five chapels dedicated to Our Lady of the Rosary, Our Lady of La Salette, Our Lady of Victories, Our Lady of Mount Carmel, and Our Lady of Pontmain. On the right side of the church, engraved in marble, is the official statement of Bishop Laurence recognizing the authenticity of the apparitions. Decorating the other walls are marble plaques and little hearts with inscriptions of the great favors received by multitudes of pilgrims through the years. Every hour, the bells of the basilica play the "Ave Maria of Lourdes."

The crypt, the original structure built dramatically into the rock above the grotto in answer to the Lady's request for a chapel, was outgrown as soon as it was completed. It serves today as a place for group Mass and private prayer. To enter, pilgrims pass through a long corridor burrowing into the hillside. Here too the walls are covered by plaques of thanksgiving for personal graces that have been received. Above the main altar, positioned directly above the place where the Holy Virgin appeared to Bernadette, is Joseph Fabisch's 1868 sculpture of the Madonna and Child. Four side altars are dedicated to the Sacred Heart, St. Peter, St. Joseph, and St. John the Evangelist. At the St. Joseph altar is an ornate reliquary containing two ribs from the body of Bernadette Soubirous. These holy relics are processed through the town from the parish church to the grotto each year on her feast day.

The Rosary Basilica is joined to the Upper Basilica by two impressive stone ramps that encircle Rosary Square.

True to its name, this basilica honors the special prayer that Bernadette prayed with the Virgin at each apparition. Atop the dome of this impressive structure is a golden cross inside a golden crown to commemorate the ceremony of the coronation of Our Lady of Lourdes. Irish pilgrims melted their wedding rings and other pieces of gold to provide the gold plating for this artwork and are credited recently for its refurbishing. The church was built in the form of a Greek cross and was consecrated in 1901. Fifteen side chapels portray scenes of the Joyful, Sorrowful, and Glorious Mysteries of the Rosary in beautifully tiled mosaics. The building can accommodate two thousand pilgrims.

There are two chapels within the Domain. Just to the left of the Rosary Basilica stands the Chapel of St. Bernadette, adorned with a mosaic of Our Lady of Lourdes surrounded by angels and nestled between two smaller altars dedicated to St. Paschal Baylon and Our Lady of Guadeloupe. The second chapel, St. Joseph's Chapel, is a small structure built partly underground and conveniently located just off the Esplanade. It holds about 450 pilgrims and is used for private gatherings.

One of the most unusual shrines in the Domain is the Basilica of St. Pius X, an enormous underground structure in the shape of an upside-down ark. Named in honor of that pontiff, who was a contemporary of Bernadette and a man who shared a deep devotion to the Madonna of the Pyrenees, it was constructed in time to commemorate the centenary of the apparitions. The building was formally consecrated by Cardinal Roncalli (the future Pope John XXIII) on March 25, 1958, exactly one hundred years to the day of the sixteenth apparition when Our Lady revealed to Bernadette, "I am the Immaculate Conception." The purpose of the underground design was to preserve the natural environment of the grotto and its surroundings, as it would have been difficult to harmonize a large modern concrete building with the stone sanctuaries around it. At more than 175,000 square feet, enough to hold 25,000 people, it is one of the largest buildings in the world. The basilica features exceptional acoustics and is used for large gatherings such as the international Masses on Wednesdays and Sundays and the culmination of the eucharistic procession for the Blessing of the Sick. Much of the space is open to accommodate wheelchairs and stretchers, but there is ample seating available for the large celebrations that take place here. One of the key features of the basilica is a central altar, situated on top of a six-foot podium and viewable to all in attendance, with television screens for added visibility. Thirty-four banners of saints and "blesseds" from all over the world decorate the building. There is also a raised walkway around the perimeter that features the Stations of the Cross, the Mysteries of the Rosary, and the story of the eighteen apparitions, all done in Gemmail, an illuminated stained-glass art, since these "windows" are below ground.

On the other side of the Gave River in an area called the Prairie is a semicircular amphitheater known as the Church of St. Bernadette. It marks the location where the young visionary had her last meeting with the Holy Virgin, as the police by that time had barricaded the grotto. The church, which opened in 1988, can hold five thousand pilgrims and features adjacent rooms for small groups. The left side of the building houses a Eucharistic Chapel for prayer and adoration. The Prairie is sometimes used for open-air Masses and other special events, accommodating crowds as large as 300,000. Also in this section of the Sanctuary is the Tent of Adoration, where the Blessed Sacrament may be venerated, and the Water Walk, nine fountains of Lourdes spring water strategically placed along the river's edge with biblical reflections at each station.

In the spirit of penitence that is an essential part of the message of Lourdes, a Reconciliation Chapel offers pilgrims forty-eight confessionals and the ability to make the sacrament in French, Italian, Spanish, English, German, Dutch, and Polish. Housed in what was originally the first accommodation for the sick, this building was refurbished in the year 2000. Another form of penance in Catholic tradition is to pray the Stations or Way of the Cross, an opportunity to prayerfully contemplate the passion and death of Jesus Christ. There are several locations throughout Lourdes where one can perform this devotion. The most famous, however, is a series of life-size sculptures that grace the hill of the Espélugues, just above the basilicas. Bishop Laurence purchased this once barren land in 1869 as a means to preserve the quietness of the shrine. Since 1912, a dramatic portrayal of Christ's historic journey to Calvary has been erected atop the rugged hill rising almost five thousand feet. The realistic figures are made of cast iron overlaid with bronze and are situated along a winding path nearly one mile in length.

Beyond the boundaries of the Domain, pilgrims will find other popular points of interest. Tours enable pilgrims to walk in the footsteps of Bernadette by visiting her early homes, the Boly Mill and *Le Cachot*; the hospice in which she served with the Sisters of Nevers; the rectory door on which she knocked to deliver her message to Abbé Peyramale; the new parish church; and Batrès, where young Bernadette tended children and sheep.

In fulfillment of the Lady's desire for a procession, two special ceremonies are held in Lourdes each day from April through October. The first is the Blessed Sacrament

Procession, a veneration of the Body, Blood, Soul, and Divinity of Christ present within the Eucharist. The procession begins at the Open-Air Altar across the Gave from the grotto at 5:00 p.m. It is led by a colorful display of pilgrimage banners, followed by pilgrims with illness and disability, by the able-bodied pilgrims, and then by the Eucharist processed by the priests under a canopy. The procession moves slowly through the Domain, across the river, past the Crowned Statue and down the esplanade to the underground Basilica of St. Pius X. Here, the multitude gathers and adores the Blessed Sacrament placed on the central altar for all to venerate. The Eucharist is then processed slowly around the altar for a Blessing of the Sick, with the medical director and other physicians following close behind, carefully observing the congregation for any signs of spontaneous healings.

Three of the physicians from our pilgrimage group were privileged to escort the Eucharist during our stay in Lourdes. For all of them, it was a tremendously moving experience.

Dr. Michael Martinelli, a cardiologist from Albany, New York, shares his experience. "I was fortunate to accompany the Blessed Sacrament during the Blessing of the Sick. I am certain my colleagues would agree that, although difficult to describe, the experience was both awesome and humbling. Being a witness to hundreds of spiritual "healings" (including my own), which could only occur with an open heart and in the Real Presence of Christ in the Eucharist, is a true "miracle" of Lourdes. The expressions of awe and profound joy to be in the presence of the Eucharist in such a holy place seemed to transcend any physical affliction."

"Processing behind the Holy Eucharist during the Blessing of the Sick was a very powerful experience," recalls

Dr. Ed Santos, a pathologist from Galesburg, Illinois. "As physicians, our goal is to make the patient get well or feel well or at least look well with the help of knowledge in the field of science and medicine. [But in Lourdes,] at that particular moment, the healing was beyond human comprehension, at least mine. It was so spiritual and divine. As I looked at the Blessed Sacrament being raised in front of the sick, I felt the inner joy that emanated from each person. That experience actually made my profession reach its completion by combining the humble human knowledge of science with the enormous intervention of the Divine. I was so touched by the turn of events. I never expected to take part in such a momentous occasion."

Dr. Linda Satterlee, a family physician from Orleans, Michigan, concurs. "The Eucharistic Procession was the most holy and spiritual experience I have ever had. As a physician, I was directed to join the other doctors in procession near the altar of the underground basilica, where thousands of pilgrims in wheelchairs and on stretchers had already processed. I felt so humbled to be walking with these physicians from all over the world, and as I looked ahead I could see the priests carrying Our Lord past the throngs of people. I felt a strong sense of oneness with all of these people, with the sick and with my colleagues who have been given the gift of practicing medicine. I then knelt in a pew to adore the Blessed Sacrament with a feeling of overwhelming joy. As I prayed, someone nudged me gently and said in French, 'Come.' I looked up to find Dr. Theillier asking me out of the pew. I stood up and realized that I was being asked to escort the priest who was to bless the sick with the Blessed Sacrament. I felt overcome with emotion and so unworthy as I walked with a colleague and with two other doctors from France and Italy. As the priest blessed the sick, I felt a tremendous energy. It was like a warmth that emanated from the Host to those being blessed and back to us. I saw people overcome with joy, healing, relief, and peace, to the point of uttering sighs. It was as though I could actually feel their healing. It felt very powerful, whether it was physical, emotional, or spiritual. Truly, I have never felt such joy."

The second important ceremony that takes place at Lourdes is the Torchlight Procession. It commences at 9:00 p.m., as twilight settles on the mountainous region, with the sound of welcome in six languages. It is a moving experience to witness a multitude of pilgrims from all corners of the earth gathering in one accord. They hold high in their hands lighted votive candles as a sign of their Baptism that have been lit from a common paschal candle. Together, the pilgrims pray and sing the Mysteries of the Rosary in a diversity of language and a unity of spirit. The slow-moving procession of glowing light travels from the grotto down the Esplanade and congregates in Rosary Square in front of the basilicas. Here the ceremony is concluded with the Salve Regina, various prayers, and Benediction, after which the pilgrims quietly disperse.

The shrine continues to undergo important new developments to commemorate the 150th anniversary of the apparitions at Lourdes. Monsignor Jacques Perrier, bishop of Tarbes and Lourdes, took time to review with me some of these changes. For example, in anticipation of the jubilee year, the baths, water taps, and other areas of the Sanctuary are being refurbished. Access to the grotto has been improved for all pilgrims, and traffic has been diverted to maintain an atmosphere of silence and reflection. In addition, a new Way of the Cross by Hungarian sculptress Maria de Faykod is being installed for the particular benefit of pilgrims physically unable to negotiate the steep climb up the hillside. While there already exists an accessible Way of the Cross on the far side of the Gave, it is not conveniently located. The new Stations will be much more prominent and more accessible for everyone.

Another important renovation is that the Rosary Basilica is being updated with the new Luminous Mysteries of the Rosary in honor of Pope John Paul II. Priest-artist Father Marco Ivan Rupnik, known for his work in the French College in Rome and the Redemptoris Mater Chapel in the Vatican, has been selected for the project. The new tiled mosaics will feature a slightly more contemporary attitude and will be installed on the three cupolas and the four pillars in the center of the basilica.

Changes are also occurring in the area of hospitality. While the fundamental concept of service performed with charity and humility remains consistent at Lourdes, a few recent innovations in the provision of volunteerism are being made to meet the needs of the times. One of these has been the creation of a new service for information dissemination. It consists of teams of two people, easily recognized in their attire, that circulate the Sanctuary and avail themselves to be questioned by visitors needing directions or other assistance. As the bishop describes, it will be a sort of mobile reception service. The new volunteer service was created to serve the anticipated crowds of the jubilee year as well as to answer a permanent and growing need at the Sanctuary. Despite what some secular media have printed, pilgrimage to Lourdes continues to grow steadily. In particular, growth is seen in the number of individual pilgrims, families, and small groups arriving at Lourdes. It is with these visitors in mind that the new mobile information service was created.

Another change is the new uniform worn by Lourdes volunteers. "There are two reasons for the recent change in uniforms for Our Lady of Lourdes Hospitality," explains the bishop. "The first is that before, the *bretelles*, or leather straps traditionally worn by Hospitality members had a use—the men who wore them used to put the handles of the stretchers through the straps to carry the sick. Now, these straps are no longer useful. They don't mean anything to people anymore. The second reason is that volunteers are now no longer just men, but men and women. Women do not traditionally carry the sick, so again the straps have no meaning. A year ago the Hospitality of Our Lady of Lourdes changed their uniform to a simple blue vest. The change has gone smoothly and quickly without any problem. At first, some people said you couldn't change the uniform because of tradition. I agree, tradition is important, but it shouldn't take precedence over service."

The transportation of special-needs pilgrims to Lourdes is another matter currently under review. Bishop Perrier and Jean-Pierre Artinagave, the mayor of Lourdes, have met with representatives of European transport and pilgrimage organizations to seek joint commitment for making travel for pilgrims with illness and disability as convenient and comfortable as possible. The plan includes converting traditional railway cars into modern ambulance carriages. "If you read the history about the transportation of the sick to Lourdes you'll see there have always been problems," says the bishop. "But the situation in recent times has gotten worse. In France, there are two kinds of trains, the high-speed trains and the older local trains, or the *corail*. We are unable to put the coach for sick people in the high-speed trains. Therefore, we have to use the older trains, and the problem is that there are fewer of them left. When you travel from Paris to Lourdes, for example, there are three or four high-speed trains. But there is only one *corail* that makes the same journey. Another problem is the fees you have to pay to transport the sick to Lourdes. These have increased a lot. Before, the train was the most economical way of transporting the sick. Now this is no longer true. The price increases have affected other countries even more than France."

While the physical changes taking place at the shrine are important, Bishop Perrier has a broader area of focus as the Sanctuary approaches its jubilee year. It is imperative in his opinion that the jubilee be oriented toward the future rather than a mere commemoration of the past. Instead of thinking about Lourdes as an isolated entity, he is interested in looking at the bigger picture of how the Church will evangelize in the world and how Lourdes can be helpful in this greater mission. In answer to this, Bishop Perrier has initiated twelve special missions that will be explored during the jubliee year, each of which gives focus to particular areas in which Lourdes has achieved competence. The twelve missions concern the sick, people with disabilities, young people, peace, Marian spirituality, conversion, the Eucharist, hospitality, the marginalized, internationality, ecumenism, and interreligious dialogue. Each of these missions has been assigned to an appropriate organization for further investigation.

The mission of the Church in relation to the sick. The sick have always had a privileged place in Lourdes since the very beginning. The care of the sick is also one of the priorities of the Church. The Italian association UNITALSI, specializing in bringing the sick to Lourdes, has been selected to explore these questions: What is the place of the sick in society and in the Church? What kind of healing can the sick who come to Lourdes hope for? Is there a Christian spirituality of illness?

The mission of the Church in relation to people with disabilities. Whether physical, mental, or both, disabilities can occur at birth or be thrust upon us suddenly during our lifetime. People with these special needs have always been a special focus of Lourdes. HCPT, a British organization specializing in taking them to Lourdes, has been asked to reflect on their place in society and in the Church, and the healing they can hope for at Lourdes.

The mission of the Church in relation to young people. Bernadette was a youth at the time of her apparitions. Youth have always been attracted to Lourdes for its diversity of peoples and the opportunity to make friendships in the service of helping pilgrims. The Fraternel, the pilgrimage group for the youth in the region of Paris, together with Boy Scouts and Girl Scouts from around the world, have been entrusted with this mission. In particular, they will consider the following: Why does Lourdes speak to young people? What do we know about young people beyond simplified clichés? What role can we play in announcing the Gospel to young people?

The mission of the Church in relation to peace. France is no stranger to the sufferings and wounds engendered by war. Lourdes, for many, has become a fortress for peace. The International Military Pilgrimage that takes place in Lourdes every year brings soldiers together to pray side by side. Many have fought against one another in history or are still in conflict. Therefore, the International Military Pilgrimage has been entrusted with these reflections: Can I truly call myself a peacemaker? With so many conflicts tearing the world apart, how do they concern me? Before taking Communion, we give each other the Sign of Peace. What is the meaning of this gesture?

The mission of the Church in relation to Mary. Mary is the perfect disciple. She is one of the facets of the Good News that must be announced to the world today, and Lourdes must fulfill its role in relation to this mission. The Montfortan Pilgrimage and the Rosary Pilgrimage have been chosen to examine the following: How does Mary speak to us? What are the distortions of Marian spirituality? What are our inadequacies in our relation to Mary?

The mission of the Church in relation to the call for conversion. Bernadette, beginning with her acts of penance in the grotto and ending with her holy death, offered her whole life for the conversion of sinners. Although this is not the most popular aspect of the message of Lourdes, all of us are called to that same spirit of conversion. At Lourdes, people find the strength in prayer and in the sacraments to begin that process. The Religious Communities of Lourdes have been called on to spearhead this mission and consider the following: People say that we have lost the sense of sin. What exactly is sin? Can we put a positive value to penance? Do we prefer certain celebrations of the Sacrament of Reconciliation, for example, as a community or as a personal act?

The mission of the Church in relation to the promotion of the Eucharist. Lourdes is as much a Eucharistic Sanctuary as it is a Marian Sanctuary. It is known for the diversity of its celebrations, from the majestic international Masses to the discreet nocturnal Masses at the grotto. The French National Pilgrimage has been assigned this particular mission and these reflections: What is the connection for us between Mary and the Eucharist? What is the connection for us between the Eucharist and serving our brothers? How can the many Christians, who call themselves Catholics without participating in the Eucharist, regain a desire for it?

The mission of the Church in relation to the service of others. Bernadette entered the convent of the Sisters of Charity and Christian Instruction in Nevers to serve the sick and the needy, and she was a remarkable nurse despite her own illness. Although not everyone is called to the religious life, each of us can make room in our lives to respond to Jesus' call to love one another through our time, talent, and treasure. The Second International Meeting of the Hospitality has been asked to explore these thoughts: It is said, more is received than is given when we serve others. Have we experienced this? What conditions are required so that volunteer service is effective for others and not just something to satisfy our consciences? How can volunteering help us to grow in or discover our Christian faith?

The mission of the Church in relationship to the marginalized. The Soubirous family was certainly marginalized, but God did not abandon them. God entrusts us to one another to build a more fraternal earth. This is the motto of the town of Lourdes. The Pilgrimage of the Traveling People has been asked to reflect on the following: Bernadette is likable to us now, but how would we have reacted at the time? Who are the "Bernadettes" and "Soubirous" of today? What are our expectations of the Church's role in this area and what is our own responsibility?

The mission of the Church in relation to the nations. The international dimension of Lourdes is very old, as pilgrim banners hanging in the museum can testify. The idea of globalization today frightens many people, especially those in the wealthiest countries. But globalization does not automatically mean the suppression of national or regional differences.

Lourdes offers the opportunity to experience the world and its diversity in one place. The Pilgrimage of the Order of Malta, a well-known international organization, has been given the task to consider these questions: What are our fears and our hopes in the face of globalization? What is the role of the Catholic Church in relation to this question? What could Lourdes do to deserve, even more so, the name of "crossroads of the world"?

The mission of the Church in relation to the unity of Christians. Catholics make up, by far, the majority of pilgrims who come to Lourdes, but many non-Catholic Christians have also been welcomed here. Mary, after all, does not belong exclusively to Catholics. All Christians love and venerate her, as she is an integral part of the Gospels. Pilgrimages composed of Catholic and Protestant Christians will be asked to explore this area: Do we consider the search for unity to be one of the compulsory missions of the Church? What do we understand about the attitudes of other Christian Communities in relation to Mary? How can Mary contribute to the unity of Christians, when she was accused of being a cause of division?

The mission of the Church in relation to interreligious dialogue. Lourdes also welcomes believers from other religions. The shrine has been visited by Muslims as well as Hindus, including the Dalaï Lama. The simple rites of drinking the water of the spring or bathing in the baths, venerating the rock of the grotto or lighting a candle have specific meaning for Christians but are not meaningless for other believers. Several diocesan pilgrimages that have among their ranks a fair number of pilgrims belonging to various religious traditions have been targeted for this mission. They will be asked to look specifically at the interreligious attraction of Lourdes and discuss a key issue of this final mission: Why is an interreligious meeting so important today?

In addition to the twelve missions, the bishop's second area of focus is to increase awareness of Lourdes worldwide. "We are seeing the development of sanctuaries and pilgrimages becoming more popular around the world," he told me. "They are important to people. This has always been true for India, for example, but it is now becoming true for the Catholic world as well. A shrine gives the opportunity for all people, especially the poor, to express themselves. It's easier to touch the rock and drink from the spring than express one's ideas at conferences and talks."

Specifically, Bishop Perrier has initiated contact with the numerous parishes, hospitals, religious communities, and other organizations in various countries that bear names related to the apparitions, like St. Bernadette's or Our Lady of Lourdes. For many, there is no longer an understanding of their historical connections to the story of the apparitions. His plan is to inform these organizations of what is happening at the shrine without requiring people to necessarily travel there. "We would like to encourage people to celebrate the jubilee in their own places," the bishop explained. "That's why I've been sending Father Régis-Marie de La Teyssonnière all over the world, to inform people about Lourdes and to enable people to make a pilgrimage to Lourdes in their hearts."

Father Régis-Marie de La Teyssonnière had an unusual break in his busy travel schedule to share with me what he has witnessed firsthand regarding the global impact of Bernadette and her apparitions. "What makes Lourdes different from other shrines is its universality," he said. "Lourdes is for all people, for all times, and it has been that way since the very beginning. Consider, for example, that Lourdes had only about four thousand inhabitants in 1858. By the fifteenth apparition, over ten thousand people from France and beyond had come to the grotto. This was an incredible number for the times. In those days, French was a universal language. Therefore, people on five continents could read what was happening in Lourdes through the French national papers. The impact of the apparitions became global quite quickly." The priest cites an example of one parish he visited, Our Lady of Lourdes in Brooklyn, New York. The parish was renamed in 1872, just ten years after the apparitions were approved, to honor the occasion. This shows the rapid spread of devotion to Bernadette and her apparitions on the other side of the ocean.

"As people returned home from their pilgrimage to Lourdes," he explained, "They brought back with them a reminder or souvenir of their experience—some water, some pictures, perhaps a statue of Our Lady. But it wasn't enough. They wanted others to have a taste of what they had experienced in the grotto. And so replicas of the grotto began to be constructed all over the world to give others at home the opportunity of entering into the same experience." An example is the life-size replica of the grotto built in Our Lady of Lourdes Parish in Brooklyn, New York. The replica has become a pilgrimage site in itself.

A second important impetus for the spread of the devotion to Our Lady of Lourdes resulted from the influence of European priests and religious sisters that were sent out as missionaries to evangelize other countries. These French, Spanish, and Italian priests and religious explained the Gospel using the story of Bernadette as a way to live that message. As a result, South America, China, Korea, Vietnam, the Philippines, Oceania, and New Zealand, for example, continue to have a strong devotion to Our Lady of

Lourdes today. It is a vital part of their Catholicism. The impact of the apparitions grew even stronger as bishops around the world desired to establish a presence of Our Lady of Lourdes in schools, parishes, and hospitals.

Father de La Teyssonnière is particularly enthused when he visits the Western world. "The Assumptionist priests were very influential in introducing Lourdes to countries in South America. To give you an example of their influence, in 2005 I had the privilege of witnessing hundreds of thousands of pilgrims from Argentina celebrate the feast day of Our Lady of Lourdes at various sanctuaries throughout the country. In North America and Canada, the Oblates of Mary Immaculate have done a great deal to promote devotion to Our Lady of Lourdes. I see a great deal of interest among North Americans in the story of Bernadette and her apparitions. Traveling to various American cities, for example, I am impressed at how many people from the individual parishes will come and attend a talk on Lourdes. I do not see the same enthusiasm in Europe right now. Being a believer in the Church and in the Gospel is quite important to American Catholics. I've had many people come up to me after a talk and thank me for the invitation to change their lives. They are responding to this invitation." Father de La Teyssonnière is documenting his findings on the impact of Lourdes around the world in his third book, yet untitled.

As Lourdes celebrates its third jubilee year, marking 150 years since the apparitions took place in 1858, Bishop Perrier is quick to remind people that Lourdes is not a museum. "Its function is to bring alive the message and to proclaim it to the men and women of the twenty-first century. What is important is to show that the message of

Lourdes, the message of the Gospel, offers a path of happiness to everyone now and for the future."[2]

Father Zambelli echoes this idea of Lourdes offering a path to happiness. "Many people today have lost the meaning of their lives in the fog of human experience," he ponders thoughtfully. "They do not know anymore where they come from or where they are going. It is like being lost during the night without a compass, without any reference points. Life loses its significance and interest. Lourdes, however, is a light that shines and attracts. It is one of the places on earth where we can receive the strength to go forward. Jesus Christ, the Saviour of all humanity, said He is the light of the world and all those who follow Him will not walk in darkness. His Mother, the Virgin Mary, also referred to in the liturgy as the Morning Star, lights the way to her Son at Lourdes. God wants her to be a sign of hope for all humankind."

Perhaps a final reflection is best summarized in the appearance of the Immaculate Virgin in a less-than-immaculate grotto to a child of lowly status and compromised health. In this unique encounter, God speaks through His mother in a powerful way to meet us where we are in life, in the midst of our poverty and failures. He comes to tell us that He loves us just as we are, with our successes but also with our wounds, our weaknesses, and our limitations. Furthermore, He asks us to love and serve our fellow humankind in their physical and spiritual poverty. To fully experience Lourdes, therefore—either in person or in prayer—we are invited not as tourists but as pilgrims prepared for true conversion. In this unique encounter we will discover a literal font of faith, hope, and charity to refresh and renew us all.

APPENDIX

Bernadette in Ecstasy

The artist affirmed that this portrait was drawn during one of Bernadette's ecstasies. While the drawing bears little resemblance to the photographs of Bernadette, the expression is clearly one of rapture. Indeed, it might have been the rapture itself that made capturing the details of Bernadette's face difficult.

The drawing bears no signature but only these words of dedication: "To the Countess of Geoffre, Lecomte de Noüy." It was given to the Museum of Bernadette at Nevers, by the Count de Certaínes. He received it from his mother, who had in turn received it from her parents. The colors have never been fixed, and have faded. Used with permission.

Prayer of St. Bernadette

Dearest Mother, how happy was my soul
those heavenly moments when I gazed upon you.
How I love to remember those sweet moments
spent in your presence,
your eyes filled with kindness and mercy for us!
Yes, dear Mother, your heart is so full of love for us
that you came down to earth to appear to a poor,
weak child
and conveyed certain things to her
despite her great unworthiness.
How humbled she is.
You, the Queen of Heaven and Earth, chose to use
what is weakest in the eyes of men.
O Mary, give the precious virtue of humility
to she who dares to call herself your child.
O Loving Mother, help your child resemble you
in everything and in every way.
In a word, grant that I may be a child
according to your heart and the heart of your dear son.

St. Bernadette, 1866

Note: This prayer is from Bernadette's journal, dedicated to
the Queen of Heaven and written during her days as a
member of the Sisters of Nevers. This is *not* the personal
prayer that Bernadette received during the fifth apparition.

Prayer to Our Lady of Lourdes

Mary, you showed yourself to Bernadette
in the crevice of the rock.
In the cold and gray of winter,
you brought the warmth, light and beauty
of your presence.

In the often obscure depths of our lives,
in the depth of the world where evil is so powerful,
bring hope! Return our confidence!

You are the Immaculate Conception,
come to our aid, sinners that we are.
Give us the humility to have a change of heart,
the courage to do penance.
Teach us to pray for all people.

Guide us to the source of true life.
Make us pilgrims going forward with your Church,
whet our appetite for the Eucharist,
the bread for the journey, the bread of life.

The Spirit brought about wonders in you, O Mary:
by his power, he has placed you near the Father,
in the glory of your eternal Son.
Look with kindness on our miserable bodies and hearts.
Shine forth for us, like a gentle light,
at the hour of our death.

Together with Bernadette, we pray to you, O Mary,
as your poor children.
May we enter, like her, into the spirit of the Beatitudes.
Then, we will be able, here below,
to begin to know the joy of the Kingdom of Heaven
and sing together with you:
Magnificent!

Glory to you, Virgin Mary,
blessed servant of the Lord,
Mother of God,
dwelling place of the Holy Spirit!
Amen.

Author Unknown

NOTES

Interviews

The conversations quoted in this book result from interviews with almost two dozen people. These are included in the text, attributed to the speaker, but with no numbered reference. I did this to maintain the flow and personal feel of those parts of the book and to clearly distinguish between conversations and quotations from published sources. Here are the circumstances of the interviews:

Father Régis-Marie de La Teyssonnière, author, lecturer, and world-renowned authority on Bernadette and her apparitions: personal interviews during my pilgrimage, October 8 through October 14, 2006.

Marlene Watkins, cofounder and executive director of Our Lady of Lourdes North American Volunteers: phone interview on July 24, 2006.

The following personnel at the Lourdes shrine: Monsignor Jacques Perrier, bishop of Tarbes and Lourdes; Father Patrick-Louis Desprez, general chaplain of the Hospitality Department of Our Lady of Lourdes; Dr. Patrick Theillier, medical director at Lourdes; Mr. Gabriel Barbry, former president of Hospitality; Mr. Philippe Tardy-Joubert, International Hospitality Conference coordinator; Father Liam Griffin, Father Marcel Emard Duguay, and Brother François Sainte-Marie, chaplains; Mr. Pierre Adias, communications director; Agnès Baranger in Communications; and Danielle Sempéré in Communications. These were all personal interviews conducted during my pilgrimage, October 8 through October 14, 2006.

Father Raymond Zambelli, the rector at Lourdes (who was out of the country at the time I was there): interviewed separately by e-mail, October 24, 2006.

John Howard, volunteer at Lourdes for the past thirty-six years: interview via telephone, June 15, 2006.

Vittorio Micheli, recipient of one of the miracles authenticated by the Church: e-mail interview through an interpreter, October 21, 2006.

Dr. Michael Martinelli, cardiologist in Albany, New York; Dr. Ed Santos, pathologist from Galesburg, Illinois; and Dr. Linda Satterlee, family physician from Orleans, Michigan—these three physicians visited Lourdes as part of the same pilgrim group I was with. E-mail interviews were conducted after our return home, to get their personal reactions to being present at the Blessing of the Sick. Their e-mail comments arrived on October 24, 2006 (Dr. Santos); October 25 (Dr. Martinelli); and November 6 (Dr. Satterlee).

I greatly regret not being able to interview Father René Laurentin, considered the world's official historian of Bernadette and the apparitions. At the time of my pilgrimage, Father. Laurentin was ninety-six years old and in poor health.

Print References

CHAPTER 1

1. René Laurentin, *Bernadette Speaks: A Life of Saint Bernadette Soubirous in Her Own Words* (Boston: Pauline Books and Media, 2000), 9.

CHAPTER 2

1. René Laurentin, *Bernadette of Lourdes: A Life Based on Authentic Documents* (Minneapolis: Winston Press, 1979), 27–28.

2. Ibid., 51.

3. Frances Parkinson Keyes, *Bernadette of Lourdes: Shepherdess, Sister, and Saint* (New York: Julian Messner, Inc., 1953), 35.

4. www.catholicpilgrims.com: reference at http://www.catholicpilgrims.com/lourdes/bd_lourdes_ apparitions.htm.

5. René Laurentin, *Bernadette Speaks: A Life of Saint Bernadette Soubirous in Her Own Words* (Boston: Pauline Books and Media, 2000), 119.

CHAPTER 3

1. René Laurentin and Bernard Billet, *Lourdes: Documents Authentiques*, quoted in Ruth Harris, *Lourdes: Body and Spirit in the Secular Age* (New York: Viking, 1999), 132.

2. Frances Parkinson Keyes, *Bernadette of Lourdes: Shepherdess, Sister, and Saint* (New York: Julian Messner, Inc., 1953), 75.

3. René Laurentin, *Bernadette Speaks: A Life of Saint Bernadette Soubirous in Her Own Words* (Boston: Pauline Books and Media, 2000), 229.

4. René Laurentin, *Bernadette of Lourdes: A Life Based on Authentic Documents* (Minneapolis: Winston Press, 1979), 137.

5. René Laurentin, *Bernadette Speaks: A Life of Saint Bernadette Soubirous in Her Own Words* (Boston: Pauline Books and Media, 2000), 460.

6. René Laurentin, *Bernadette of Lourdes: A Life Based on Authentic Documents* (Minneapolis: Winston Press, 1979), 231.

7. René Laurentin, *Bernadette Speaks: A Life of Saint Bernadette Soubirous in Her Own Words* (Boston: Pauline Books and Media, 2000), 531.

CHAPTER 4

1. René Laurentin, *Bernadette of Lourdes: A Life Based on Authentic Documents* (Minneapolis: Winston Press, 1979), 217.

CHAPTER 5

1. Ruth Harris, *Lourdes: Body and Spirit in the Secular Age* (New York: Viking, 1999), 280.
2. Ibid., 322.

CHAPTER 6

1. Patricia A. McEachern, *A Holy Life* (San Francisco: Ignatius Press, 2005), 38.
2. René Laurentin, *Bernadette of Lourdes: A Life Based on Authentic Documents* (Minneapolis: Winston Press, 1979), 187–88.
3. René Laurentin, *Bernadette Speaks: A Life of Saint Bernadette Soubirous in Her Own Words* (Boston: Pauline Books and Media, 2000), 167.
4. Ibid., 541–42.
5. Patrick Marnham, *Lourdes: A Modern Pilgrimage* (New York: Doubleday, Image Books, 1982), 171–72.
6. Frances Parkinson Keyes, *Bernadette of Lourdes: Shepherdess, Sister, and Saint* (New York: Julian Messner, Inc., 1953), 138.
7. www.mike.friese.com/pilgrimage/paris/bernaut.html 9/18/06.

8. Benedict J. Groeschel, CFR, *A Still, Small Voice: A Practical Guide on Reported Apparitions* (San Francisco: Ignatius Press, 1993), 150.

CHAPTER 7

1. Patrick Theillier, *Talking About Miracles* (Cambridge, UK: Redemptorist Publications, 2003), 82.

2. Ibid., 91.

3. Patrick Theillier, "Procedure for Recognition of Cures in Lourdes," *Fons Vitae: Bulletin of the Medical Bureau of Lourdes* (July 2006): 5.

4. Monsignor Jacques Perrier, "Today's Position on Miracles," *Lourdes Magazine*, no. 130 (142), April–May 2006: 10.

5. Pawel Zuchniewicz, *Miracles of John Paul II* (Toronto: Catholic Youth Studio-KSM Inc., 2006), 86–87.

CHAPTER 8

No notes.

CHAPTER 9

1. René Laurentin, *Bernadette of Lourdes: A Life Based on Authentic Documents* (Minneapolis: Winston Press, 1979), 168.

2. Mathias Terrier, "A Generosity of a Thousand Faces," *Lourdes Magazine*, no. 129 (141), March–April 2006: 18.

CHAPTER 10

1. Lourdes-France.org Web site, July 11, 2006 http://www.lourdes-france.org/index.php?goto_centre=ru&contexte=en&id=563.

2. Catholic News Service, February 11, 2005 http://www.catholicnews.com/data/stories/cns/0500858.htm.

3. Catholic World News, August 16, 2004 http://www.buzztracker.org/2004/08/17/cache/310520.html.

4. Pawel Zuchniewicz, *Miracles of John Paul II* (Toronto: Catholic Youth Studio-KSM Inc., 2006), 85.

5. Lourdes-France.org Web site, August 8, 2006 http://www.lourdes-france.org/index.php?goto_centre=ru&contexte=en&id=838.

6. Linda de Plazaola, "Cured in Lourdes, She Becomes a Hospitalier with the Rosary Pilgrimage," *Lourdes Magazine*, no. 133 (145), September–October 2006: 36.

CHAPTER 11

1. *The Official Guide of the Sanctuary*, 2006: 9–10.

2. The Official Site of the 150th Anniversary of the Apparitions http://www.lourdes2008.com/index_en.html.

BIBLIOGRAPHY

Books

Groeschel, Benedict J., CFR. *A Still, Small Voice: A Practical Guide on Reported Apparitions*. San Francisco: Ignatius Press, 1993.

Harris, Ruth. *Lourdes: Body and Spirit in the Secular Age*. New York: Viking, 1999.

Keyes, Frances Parkinson. *Bernadette of Lourdes: Shepherdess, Sister, and Saint*. New York: Julian Messner, Inc., 1953.

Laurentin, René. *Bernadette of Lourdes: A Life Based on Authentic Documents*. Minneapolis: Winston Press, 1979.

————. *Bernadette Speaks: A Life of Saint Bernadette Soubirous in Her Own Words*. Boston: Pauline Books and Media, 2000.

Marnham, Patrick. *Lourdes: A Modern Pilgrimage*. Garden City, New York: Doubleday, Image Books, 1982.

Martin, Sally. *Every Pilgrim's Guide to Lourdes*. Norwich, UK: Canterbury Press, 2005.

McEachern, Patricia A. *A Holy Life*. San Francisico: Ignatius Press, 2005.

Theillier, Patrick. *Talking About Miracles*. Cambridge, UK: Redemptorist Publications, 2003.

Zuchniewicz, Pawel. *Miracles of John Paul II*. Toronto: Catholic Youth Studio-KSM Inc., 2006.

Other Publications

de Plazaola, Linda. "Cured in Lourdes, She Becomes a Hospitalier with the Rosary Pilgrimage." *Lourdes Magazine*, no. 133 (145), September–October 2006: 36.

Perrier, Monsignor Jacques. "Today's Position on Miracles." *Lourdes Magazine*, no. 130 (142), April–May 2006: 10.

Terrier, Mathias. "A Generosity of a Thousand Faces." *Lourdes Magazine*, no. 129 (141), March–April 2006: 18.

Theillier, Patrick. "Procedure for Recognition of Cures in Lourdes." *Fons Vitae: Bulletin of the Medical Bureau of Lourdes* (July 2006): 5.

The Official Guide of the Sanctuary. (2006): 9–10.

Web Sites

Catholic Encylopedia: www.newadvent.org (5/16/2006)

Catholic On-line: www.catholic.org (5/16/2006)

Catholic News Service: http://www.catholicnews.com/data/stories/cns/0500858.htm (2/11/2005)

Catholic World News: http://www.cwnews.com/news/viewstory.cfm?recnum=31509 (8/16/04)

Lourdes-france.org

Middlesborough Lourdes 2006: www.middlesboroughlourdes. co.uk (5/16/2006)

Official Site for the 150th Anniversary of the Apparitions: http://www.lourdes2008.com/en/lourdes/renommee-australie. htm (8/15/06)

Official Site of the Sanctuary of Lourdes: www.lourdes-france.com/index.php?texte=1&langage=en (5/1/2006)

Sunday Catholic Weekly: www.niedziela.pl (5/18/2006)

www.catholicpilgrims.com (5/16/2006)

www.mike.friese.com/pilgrimage/paris/bernaut.html (9/18/06)

ACKNOWLEDGMENTS

The author thanks the people and organizations who kindly gave their permission to use the following illustrations:

Cover photos

Source of the grotto's spring, by Pierre Vincent. Copyright © Sanctuaires Notre-Dame de Lourdes/EURL Basilique Rosaire.

Bernadette Soubirous, photographer unknown. Courtesy of the Congregation of the Sisters of Nevers.

Candlelight procession outside the Basilica of Lourdes, photographer unknown. Copyright © Sanctuaires Notre-Dame de Lourdes/EURL Basilique Rosaire.

Statue of the Immaculate Conception. Courtesy of Paul McMahon.

Gold crown atop the Basilica of Lourdes. Courtesy of Mark Ficocelli.

Volunteers bringing pilgrims to the grotto, by M Durand. Copyright © Sanctuaires Notre-Dame de Lourdes/EURL Basilique Rosaire.

Hands cupping water from the grotto's spring, by the author.

Interior illustrations

P. 81. Bernadette Soubirous, photographer unknown. Courtesy of the Congregation of the Sisters of Nevers.

Grotto at the time of the apparitions, by M. Viron. Copyright © Sanctuaires Notre-Dame de Lourdes/ EURL Basilique Rosaire.

P 82. Grotto at night. Courtesy of Mark Ficocelli.

Hands cupping water from Lourdes, by the author.

P. 83. Statue in the niche. Courtesy of Paul McMahon.

Votive candles, by the author.

P. 84. Plaque marking where Bernadette knelt. Courtesy of Mark Ficocelli.

Volunteer showing lifting techniques. Photo by author.

P. 85. Plaque commemorating John Paul II's visits. Courtesy of Michael Kerrigan, CSP.

Flowers at the source of the spring. Courtesy of Mark Ficocelli.

P. 86. Rosary Basilica. Courtesy of Paul McMahon.

Crown on the dome. Courtesy of Mark Ficocelli.

P. 87. Basilica. Courtesy of Mark Ficocelli.

Crowned statue. Courtesy of Paul McMahon.

P. 88. Blessed Sacrament Procession, by M. Lacaze. Copyright © Sanctuaires Notre-Dame de Lourdes/EURL Basilique Rosaire.

Thousand of volunteers, M. Durand. Copyright © Sanctuaires Notre-Dame de Lourdes/EURL Basilique Rosaire.

P. 89. Torchlight Procession, photographer unknown. Copyright © Sanctuaires Notre-Dame de Lourdes/EURL Basilique Rosaire.

Taking part in procession. Courtesy of Mark Ficocelli.

P. 90. Incorrupt body, photographer unknown. Courtesy of the Congregation of the Sisters of Nevers.

Statue of Bernadette with lambs. Courtesy of Michael Kerrigan, CSP.

P. 166. *Bernadette in Ecstasy*. Pastel, artist unknown, ca. 1858. Pastel signed "Lecomte of Noüy dedicated to the Countess of Joffre." Given by Mr. Étienne of Some to the Museum of Bernadette at Nevers. Courtesy of the Congregation of the Sisters of Nevers.